TELEGONOS
A Tragedy in Verse

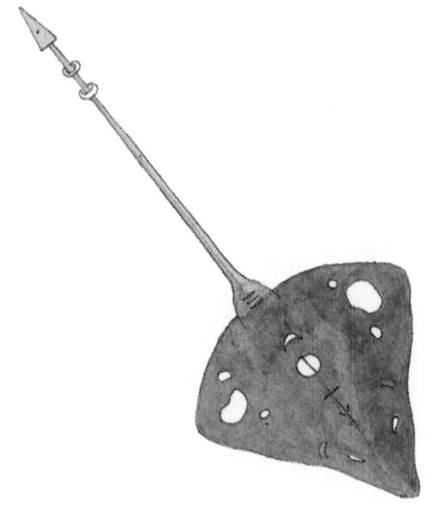

JONATHAN GOLDING

DARKLY BRIGHT PRESS

Telegonos: A Tragedy in Verse
by Jonathan Golding

Telegonos: A Tragedy in Verse:
© 2021 by Jonathan Golding. *All rights reserved.*

Interior Art:
© 2021 by Megan Gilbert. *All rights reserved.*
www.megan-gilbert.com

Foreword: © 2021 by Gaelan Gilbert. *All rights reserved.*

Graphics and book design:
© 2021 by Christopher Tompkins. *All rights reserved.*

Cover illustration:
San Ponziano in an Amphitheatre Being Exposed to Lions
by Christopher Unterberger

Catalog Number 012

ISBN: 978-1-7331964-6-8

Library of Congress Control Number: 2021944203

**darkly bright
press & design**

www.darklybrightpress.com

TELEGONOS

Foreword by Gaelan Gilbert	7
Dramatis Personae	11
ACT I	15
ACT II	35
ACT III	55
ACT IV	81
ACT V	101

Foreword

Years ago, I was camping in a wilderness area on the western coast of North America, in a place far distant from any city. It was a moonless night, and the sky was dark, except for a few wispy clouds. All of a sudden, a blazing light coursed across the dome of night, tracing a bright tail and dispelling the darkness. The shooting star—alive with movement—seemed to stop time. It was a profoundly beautiful experience that I was not expecting. It was one I cannot forget.

This is, frankly, how I felt the first time I immersed myself in the book you hold in your hands. Reading Jonathan Golding's **TELEGONOS** seemed to stop time. To read it was to enter into another world, one I had only encountered in texts authored centuries ago. It was a recognizable world, replete with elements that anyone familiar with Sophocles or Shakespeare, let alone Homer, will greet with pleasure. But its natural and seamless admixture of all three—this was a surprise. One I'll not forget.

TELEGONOS is a unique treasure, a jewel which can be viewed from many angles. It is at once an imaginative extension of Homer's Odyssey with ingenious additions in a dramatic form; a plot-driven and character-forging quest in a Tempest-like setting of coastal cliffs and ancient enchantments; a layering of story within story; a panoply of mysterious symbolism and foreshadowing dreams; a tragic tale about the fixed fact of ignorant fate; a concrete experiment of freedom, chance, hope, and healing; a blend of manifold pre-modern sensibilities with the benefit of hindsight from twenty-first century literary history; and much more.

In a recent study of fiction and narrative, theologian John Milbank evokes the "the drained desert of money, machinery, and electronic signals" in which we find ourselves at this stark stage of modern history. In such a desert, which is a godless place, a work like Golding's **TELEGONOS** is a refreshing oasis, fulfilling one of art's two Horatian purposes: delight. But, in the way that all great literature does, Golding's work also illumines and instructs. It casts the image of truth in its allure and the spectre of falsity in its ugliness. It populates the imagination (and thus memory) with figures whose virtues and flaws assume mythic if recognizable proportions. It rediscovers the undeniable mystery of time and the layers of felt experience which both distinguish and connect past, present, and future. Finally, it explores the invisible realm of realities that are no less real for being spiritual or symbolic, and how that realm inhabits and in-forms our visible environs.

Milbank closes his study by speculating that "the belief in God and in the triune God can perhaps only be revived if we re-envisage and re-imagine the immanent enchantments of the divine creation which appropriately witnesses to the transcendent One through a polytheistic profusion of created enigmas." I could hardly think of a better way to describe Golding's dramatic debut. **TELEGONOS** exemplifies the great spiritual potential that fiction has today.

Gaelan Gilbert

Gaelan Gilbert is an adjunct professor of Literature & History at Hellenic College in Brookline, MA, and Visiting Professor of Arts & Humanities at the University of Saint Katherine in San Diego, CA. He has studied and taught in parts of Europe and North America. His poetry has appeared here and there. He lives with his wife and their four children in New York. He is the author of a collection of poetry, *One Is Found First* (Darkly Bright Press, 2018) and a children's book, *Laurel and the Wind* (Ancient Faith, 2020).

TELEGONOS

A Tragedy in Verse

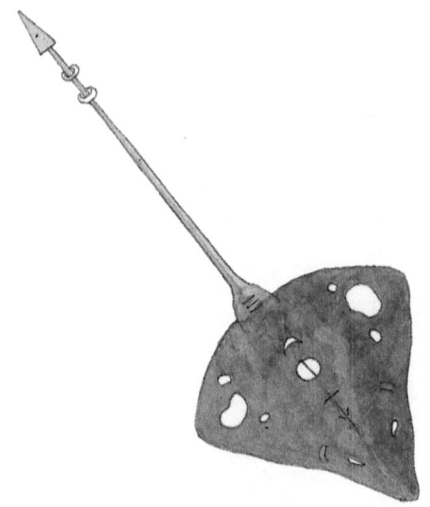

JONATHAN GOLDING

DARKLY BRIGHT PRESS

Dramatis Personae

Polysemous: A servant to Prince Telegonos

Xanthicus: A young fisherman

Old Man: A mysterious aged figure

Telegonos: A youthful prince, the son of the goddess Circe, and King Odysseus

Caissa: A shepherdess

Diotima: A shepherdess

Calidus: A soldier and servant to King Odysseus

Callimachus: A soldier and servant to King Odysseus

Odysseus: The king of Ithaca

Captain: A commander of the army of Ithaca

1st Soldier: A soldier of Ithaca

2nd Soldier: A soldier of Ithaca

Scout: A soldier of Ithaca

Penelope: Queen of Ithaca

Kalonous: A nobleman of Thrace and companion to Telegonos

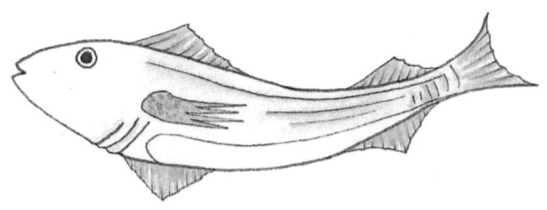

ACT I

TELEGONOS, ACT I

Scene: *A sea cliff and strand on Ithaca. In the cliff wall, a cave with stone steps leading up to it. Above, a ledge with numerous rocky paths. At left, an olive tree. Toward center, a spring. Polysemous is discovered alone on stage gathering firewood.*

Polysemous: One, two, and three, and kindling will make fire.
I'll rest a time and then collect another load.
Will be an easy task since many scraps lie scattered close.
See, here's a bit of splintered plank has washed
Up on the beach, and there a rib of ship
Or shattered spar cast up to bleach and season
For a length beneath the endless sun.

How freight the rising tide today with
Scantling fragments of our late disaster!
Most plain these timbers tell of our misfortune,
That black typhoon, which with a vast disorder,
Convulsed the ocean face we travelled on
And thefted us, in one, of vessel and our arms,
Provisions, friends, and all that we possessed.

Ho, here's a find! A cookpot drawn by sheeting surf
Most to the print and pattern of my feet!
Can it be sound? I see no fret, nor trace a crack.
Ha! That's as lovely and as good a music
As ever in my days 'til now I've heard.
Come, my friend, and I will jig you to a spring
And wash you of this griming coat of time.
Soon you'll serve me by my fire to brew
A stew or cauldron up some fresh caught game.

[A cry offstage.]

Listen! My master, Prince Telegonos,
Cries out in visions of his slumbering.
Yet scarcely can I call it by the name of sleep,
For though he lingers in the house of Death's
More welcome elder kinsman, no comfort,
Nor rest, nor peace he finds there in those halls,
But journeys with protracted steps, enmazed
In fierce dark windings of some fevered dream.

How deep, how mutable a mystery
Lies fast and hid within the sea's wide wild heart!
Not four days past were these bright waters changed,
Grew livid, as with a spreading bruise.
Then the heart within me died as failing
And so frail seemed all the seacraft of all men
Before that charged and swelling strength of sea.
Yet now, it shines as peaceful as an hour!
And who may say which vision is deceives?
There is no rest or permanence in earth
Or sky or sea, but all is constant flux.
And the good cheats through our fingers like sand.
[Xanthicus is heard singing offstage.]
But, hear now! What careless song is this,
That down the beach abrupts the early stillness?
Perhaps some islander goes singing to his trade.
Within a fracture of the rock I'll hide myself
To covert view what chance shall bring my way.
Perhaps from ash our fortunes may arise again.

[Xanthicus enters singing at left. While in song he spies the spring and goes to it to fill his jug.]

Song: *Hey ho! Hey ho!*
        What a bundle of fish I have!
        What a bundle of fish I have!
        I'll sort the good for market day,
        And throw the bad away.
        And throw the bad away.
        Hey ho! Hey ho!
        I fished all night, but had no luck.
        I fished all night, but had no luck.
        But with the dawning day,
        The fish jumped in my net!
        The fish jumped in my net!
        I'll sort the good for market day,
        And throw the bad away.
        And throw the bad away.

[He breaks off a branch of the olive tree and makes a mark in the sand.]

TELEGONOS, ACT I   17

Xanthicus: Here now, at last, is water and a bit
Of wood to mark my way. No more of care!
I'll find my skiff and tack the windward home!

Polysemous: Oh, stay, good youth, and heed a suppliant!

Xanthicus: Ai! Ai! Ah!

Polysemous: What is this now? Rise up. Why do you cower there?

Xanthicus: I'm not—Ah, no! Do not strike me with your curse!
I would not be a beast! It is too much for any man to bear it!

Polysemous: What are these mad, unmanful cries?
I speak no threats. Be easier of purpose.

Xanthicus: I have but come to fill this breaker's empty store.

Polysemous: You still mistake me. In other sort I spoke.

Xanthicus: Your words were plain. I've told you all my task.
Stay back! Come not so close. I fear your hand!

Polysemous: It is empty.

Xanthicus: Your touch, then, your touch!

Polysemous: How strange your talk. I know not what to make of it.
Come; take back your mantle from before your eyes.
Look well, and see I am no dark-faced ghost,
Nor one who lives by plunder or by brigandage.

Xanthicus: I would go, sir! Please, do let me go!

Polysemous: Why? What in apprehension do I seem?

Xanthicus: A man. Only a man in tattered cloak.
But seeming is not always so, I've found.

Polysemous: A true philosophy, but false in this.
For stands before you now no outlaw,

But one made wretched by a wretched fate.
Do not be frightened so.

Xanthicus: 'Most do your gentle words
Persuade me.

Polysemous: Our fears are sometimes lies.

Xanthicus: But often they say true.

Polysemous: Come, rise. Persuade yourself to manfulness,
And you may hear a word to your advantage.

Xanthicus: I will attend you.

Polysemous: I am a man by sad
Calamity and by some warp of fortune
Cast forth the sea and alien to this shore.

Xanthicus: Stranger, what is it that you wish of me?

Polysemous: I've nothing had save one scorched taro root
And leaves of ripple grass to salad on
These three days past and I grow rabbit starved.
You carry there a basket full of fish.

Xanthicus: Basket? Fish? Ho, yes my fish! Aue!
Hard labor had I to fetch them forth the sea.

Polysemous: As is the custom of my people,
I have within my hair a binding clasp,
Worked on a shard of jasper set with gilt.
And if you will, I'll barter it against your wares.

Xanthicus: I've never seen its like. Ha! Here appears
A wonderment! See, this one side is carved
In image of a lowly insect that devours,
But when I turn it on my open palm
Another shape discovers to my sight,
Some human form that skies aloft on wings.

Polysemous: It far exceeds the worth these simple wares,
But what are trinkets to a man in need?

Xanthicus: Good fortune, sir! For this, you'll have the lot.

Polysemous: Good then. Come now,
And sit here at this friendly warmth of fire.
To this wild and shifting world, I am in name
Polysemous. And you, what are you called?
And where that town to which you will return?
But most I'd have you say, what isle is this?
Three days passage have I measured here
Without one trace the fellowship of human kind.
I would now know what manner men live close,
And who is he who governs on these shores?

Xanthicus: What shoals of askings here have come to swim.
Still, I make catch by livelihood and trade.
I, Xanthicus, am called, for in this sweet
Season of the spring I celebrate my birth.
My island home lies not a day from here,
Across the turquoise and great green of sea,
And there, beneath the Mountain of Spices, I dwell.

Polysemous: Good then. I like a lad who answers straight.
Speak more.

Xanthicus: Of what?

Polysemous: Of that I did request.

Xanthicus: I have forgotten it.

Polysemous: To what broad reach
Or angle of the world have now I come?

Xanthicus: Of this country, sir, some name it this,
Some other calls it that. What matters it?
I have no wish to know it, but only fly!

Polysemous: It seems some part your early fear returns,

For here we are alone where none pursues.

Xanthicus: I'll say no more, but to this course I'm constant,
And were you wise, I'd bid you to the same.

Polysemous: How so?

Xanthicus: We both are strangers to this coast.
When you have fed, let us two get from hence.
To find my skiff and leave. This is a wicked place.

Polysemous: Be easy, Xanthicus, and tell me what you dread.

Xanthicus: It's said an evil king reigns here, who in times past
Deceived the nation's youth and drew them to his halls.
But after they had feasted and well drunk,
Like a reaper in a field of spelt,
He cut them down. And from this deadly action,
A curse and hatred of the gods has grown.
The telling man who keeps our village shrine
Repeated me this tale, and I once mocked at it.
Yet now, I'll credit truth which then I scorned.

Polysemous: What have you witnessed so to change your mind?
Come; do not be silent, but tell me in good faith.

Xanthicus: A harder task you could not lay on me.
The house of memory has many rooms,
And only the unwise go in them all.

Polysemous: Still, again, in this I would entreat you,
For it is true, as elder wisdom states,
That courage will from counsels often grow.

Xanthicus: You may then hear a shadow tale to 'maze the mind.

Polysemous: Be sure I am resolved to it. Say on.

Xanthicus: Know then, that I am usual on the bay
Of my small island home to cast my net,
But to the deep that lies beyond the land

TELEGONOS, ACT I

I yet do of a sometime turn my craft,
To hunt among the waves the rarer fish that pays.
Of yesterdawn, I put forth on such end,
But when the waves had grayed with waning light,
And I grew thirsty on the roads of the sea,
I sought the shelter of a cove here close.
Above incessant rush and language of the surf,
I heard, or thought I heard, a smoother sound
Of water over rock. To seek it out,
I made my way in copse of plane tree, pine,
And laurel. Never could I find its source,
Some shining silver wind of woodland stream,
But in the growing twilight then I glimpsed a flame.
As a one bidden, drawn to its light,
I turned my steps aside, and bending back
A pliant span of glossy leaf, I found
A field full of some ragged folk around a fire.
Then from this secret place I heard their talk.

"My friends," said one of grave deport, "we must
Decide the means and scope of our intended
Search, to know if any else has here
Survived, and most if on this wasteland shore
Our honored lord yet lives." But murmured they against
His word as I heard cry, "Let Thymos speak! Give ear!"
Then one tall and brawn of limb leapt lightly
To a mossy stone and gestured silence.
"Brothers!" cried he. "Kalonous does misprize
Our circumstance! Do you none remember
How we once were slaves of vile sorcery?
That sorrow I would burn upon your minds,
That you might learn to look on this our lot
With fresher eyes. It is, in truth, a gift,
Most heavenish and most rare, of freedom!
We can now hold our destiny and mold
It as we will. We must it safely ward,
Lest we be scattered on the reaches of the earth!"
And more he seemed about to speak, but straight
Broke off, and sudden stillness came on all,
As though oppressed by strange and soundless thunder.
Then that called Thymos, all at once, raised up

His arms before his face to dimness of the sky,
In likeness of a captive chained and pleading.
And wide the hollow of his mouth he gaped,
As fish will do when cast into a boat.
At last, into a mute and stifled air,
His tongue let loose a speechless cry of pain.
Then rushed my blood as by a pulse of wind,
And yet my gazing held me fast.
Soon came a change that larger horror holds.
For while he lunged, with torment much, his head
From side to side, an endless and unhuman
Howl erupting from the furor of his lips,
From flesh behind his ear burst forth a point
Of whitest ivory that split the flesh
And lengthened into horn. As grew its twin,
Of an instant, his features so distort became
And swelled and melted like a tallow touched by burning,
That, though in figure he remained a man,
All mannishness of countenance he lost,
And stood now crowned in aspect like a bull.
Then dropped he down and I saw not the more
Of his sad alteration 'til the crowd
In panic parted and revealed a beast complete.

Oh, that my eyes were stones that cannot see!
For how can I relate what came the next?
As scattered they, like hectic autumn leaves,
That in confusion circle and are caught
In churning, turning, restless tides of wind,
Each all some liking lapse bore in his way.
Look on with eyes of heart if you can dare
And witness one, who stumbles to the mold,
His face in ruins, that lies with heaving flanks.
See the bloat, shudder, ripple, merge of flesh,
As he becomes a swine, devoid of sense,
Who struggles up on hooves, to naked feast,
His only thought now pods or cobs of earth.
Or see now this sad youth with blondish beard,
Who runs with gaze distract and clutches at his heart
As though it rusted in his hollow breast,
And all consumed with vex of inly grief,

TELEGONOS, ACT I

He trips on tufts of grass and tumbles down.
Now limbs proportioned once to human use
Disform and beat against the turf in agony,
Then gather and collect, as up to spring,
A wolf of hate, voracious and malign.
Some changed to cormorants, who feed on the wealth of the sea.
Still others never rose, but shapeless bears became,
And slept with empty minds whatever place they fell.
I saw another danced a rigadoon
Of anguished steps, and witnessed I his eyes
Grow dull, and thence contract in goatish slits,
Fill up with pitiless desire, until
He had become a satyr of the wood,
Who slow thropped off, to sport in wildwood groves,
With savage mirth, as to the pipes of Pan.
But when I saw that great leviathan rise up
To overmaster all the rest, I ran
And ran, through dense, rough tangle of a pathless wood,
And lost my way. I spent the night I know not where.
Oh, aching night of dread and starting fear,
But when the day began to spring forth free,
I too came forth to find again the sea.

Polysemous: Oh, harsh! This saddest argument has touched
My nature's inmost core.

Xanthicus: And yet, how wide
The mark your secret thoughts, this sentence falls.

Polysemous: What words are these? I have but spoke my heart.

Xanthicus: It seems some cruel god or fate played guide,
When I, by wandered steps, came late to you.
I noted well the paling of your cheek
At the name of Thymos and of the other
That Kalonous they called. And of their stripe
And of their company you seem to me.
Perhaps you are that desperate chieftain
That they within the wood once thought to seek
Before they lost the good of human shape.

Polysemous: Not I, but one who lies within this cave.
I'm not a man, of custom, to nakedly unpack
The business of my lord, but since it may
Lay siege the fear that now invests your mind
I'll cast aside such prudence for the truth.
Hear then, my master, Prince Telegonos, is son
To goddess Circe and that fated wanderman,
Odysseus, who soonest came not home
From great destruction of that city Troy,
Which Priam's sire built on the Hill of Doom.

Xanthicus: Such names as these I do not know, but I
Will listen on and learn the outcome.

Polysemous: In ignorance of his true father's name,
The boy grew up in kingdom of illusion strange,
For Circe, daughter of the Sun, transforms
To beasts all those who dare transgress her bounds.
When he had fully come into a man's estate,
This prince in somewise learned his parentage,
And then desired no other thing but this,
To over sea and seek the father's kingdom far.
This wish pleased not the goddess Circe's mind,
But on his will she could no more prevail.
She loosed some remnant of her captive host
To labor and construct a ship to bear her son
Across the waves. And to this bold endeavor,
The wise Athena also lent her skill,
And caused our vessel hence to be no common craft,
But such as was endued with her immortal art.

Xanthicus: To be so aided by divinity
Soars up beyond the common lot of men.
But say what happened next in this great cause.

Polysemous: Circe chose out fifty solid men
To make this exploration on the deep
And granted freedom each that fellowship.
But with a guileful mind she made this proclamation,
For in that cargo of our provender
She mingled certain of her magic drugs,

To this effect, that all so fed on it
Might for a time retain a human shape,
But should three days pass by without its taste,
Those men should suffer a dread reversion,
Becoming beasts once more. But to myself alone,
This fact was known for she remitted me
This pain that I might act as ward to him.

It seems an age since we weighed anchor stones
To leave behind the Island of Sad Wailing,
Yet well our voyage went, 'til in the night,
A storm, with its great hand, caught hold our ship
And drove there against some spur of rock.
And I knew not 'til now others had been
Saved from the waves. For these you witnessed in the forest dense,
By saddest metamorphosis transformed,
Are but the crew of that ill fortuned ship.
And though a magic works on them, it's none
The doing of that lord who rules this land.
Just there, within the dry den of this cave
Telegonos, their prince, in sickness sleeps.

Xanthicus: He sounds, this prince, a man one could admire.

Polysemous: He may become one such if seasoned by the years,
For yet I still perceive in him a certain haste.
But I have been too long solitary
To speak these inward thoughts into your ears.
Are you now certified against dismay?

Xanthicus: I am. But see; here someone comes along the beach,
And by his rags, I'd say he's one your fellowship.

[Enter the Old Man.]

Polysemous: I know him not nor like his beggared look.
I'll speak. How fares the morning's peace, good sir?

Old Man: Ill and ever only ill, since I,
In Exile, now wander out around about
The weary margins of the weary world,

To feed on scavenge of the vengeful sea.
Still, this day is not so ill as all the rest,
For three nights since, a vessel, bound I know
Not where, ran smack aground and spilled its wealth
Upon the cranching tide. And so, from death,
I have my life, in an unequal trade.
But who are you, that come thus to the cave
Of the Kena bird, beneath the bright eye of the dawn?

Polysemous: Tell not my business, for I trust him not.

Xanthicus: But why? What harm is in such one as this?

Polysemous: He seems to me like some too cryptic colored owl
Who silent loves to hunt within the silent night.
We are fishers finding shelter in this place.
Know you then this country, ancient sire?

Old Man: Bah! I only know the pains I suffer,
The chill that beats at hands and feet and will
Not go away. To age in poverty
Is an unlovely thing. And all an old man's pleasure
Is but to warm his bones some deal of hours.

Polysemous: Some other fire, be pleased to seek, old sir,
For we have much of task in hand today.

Old Man: You do not have, by some small chance, a jug
Of wine or loaf of bread? For bread sustains
The heart of man on the journey of this life,
And old age is a dry and careful time.
The blood of grapes can light the load we bear.

Polysemous: We have no wine, old man. I say again,
Search out another place to rest your ancient cares.

Old Man: Ha, such takingness I had not thought to gaze on.

Polysemous: What's that?

Xanthicus: He looks now to the fish I caught.

TELEGONOS, ACT I

Polysemous: Old man, be gone and trouble us no more.

Xanthicus: Drive not the old one far away, my friend,
For Zeus of counsels so enjoins our love
And on the stranger ever keeps a watch,
To honor those who haven them with grace.

Polysemous: Speak not of gods to me, for well I know them.
You lack a practiced eye to judge his type.
I say again, old fool, be on your way!

Old Man: You are too hasty and too hot of heart!
Beware, lest some immortal look upon
Your wrath with an unkinder eye than mine.

Polysemous: Oh, too importunate old dog!

[A struggle ensues.]

Old Man: Help! Help!

Polysemous: I'll lesson you!

Old Man: Murder!

Xanthicus: Oh, by the gods!

[In the midst of this, Telegonos comes to the mouth of the cave above and stands a moment. While he speaks the following lines he begins descending. He is barefoot and carries an ornately carved spear.]

Telegonos: Cease now this strife!
        What does this violent outbreak mean?

Polysemous: I am abashed, my lord, and have not words.

Telegonos: No words? Never have I heard a man who flows
With so abundant sense as you. Indeed,
How like the very ocean are most times
The tidings of your talk. What would you, sir?

Old Man: I but hankered on this morsel.

Telegonos: A fish?
We have not crossed such dark salt seas for this,
To brawl like market chapmen on a scrap of cod.
Give it him and be done.

Polysemous: My thought was only to your good, my lord.

Telegonos: And for your tendment kind, I give you thanks,
And will the more when time is opportune.

Old Man: Oh, may Athena, the unwearied one,
Whose eyes are like the owl's, look down
And bless you with her good and help!

Telegonos: Know you this place?

Old Man: It's but a place, no more.

Xanthicus: They say the king is of a cunning turn
Of mind and vile.

Telegonos: Why so?

Polysemous: It seems he rules
By stealth and dark assassination's force.
And has consolidated his estate by murder.

Telegonos: A tyrant king? Then I am glad of this,
My spear, the gift of gods and thwart to all my foes.

Xanthicus: An immortal gift is rare indeed.

Telegonos: Hephaistos, god of fire, with subtle art forged this
Of bronze and ash and tipped it with the spine
Of that fierce ray that goes within the deep.
But no more this for now. This land is rugged.
How sheer these stones that time has touched rise up,
Yet when I look within, how green it seems
And like a paradise of gods unknown.

I think that here the rain must often fall.
How many of our men came safe to shore?

Polysemous: Of that I know no more than does this boy
But think not more on them for now, my Prince.

Telegonos: Not think on them!
   What word's escaped your teeth?
To be so poor in loyalty is want indeed.

Old Man: What men are these you speak on, noble sir?

Telegonos: My own. My constant crew
   who shipped with me of late
And pledged themselves in service to my person.

Old Man: Then yours that vessel wrecked three nights gone by?

Telegonos: It was.

Old Man: Ha! I knew you for no fisherman. Ha!

Polysemous: Be stilled. I am rejoiced in heart to find
You so returned in health, but listen to
A word or two, my Prince. The fire now embers low
And soon will all but out. We must secure
Our lot before we make attempt to find
Our vanished crew.

Telegonos: Some quickwork lies about;
The scattered wreckages and tokens of our loss.

Polysemous: But most is moist and will not serve the turn.

Xanthicus: A raft of timber back within
A clearing of the wold I glimpsed, just there.
Will be light labor of an hour to gather it,
For now I have no check of fear to hold me.

Telegonos: What fear? Has this wicked king
   some sentry posted close?

Polysemous: No, it's but a nothing.

Xanthicus: I was but little lost and so alarmed.

Telegonos: Your looks are strange and speak some mystery,
But I will not inquire against its cause for now.
I will be said by you, Polysemous,
First to supply these needfuls fit, and then
Hunt out the fate of friends we miss.

Polysemous: But let's divide the greater ground to go.

Telegonos: Ah!

Polysemous: What means this?

Xanthicus: He grimaces in pain.

Telegonos: A lack is here I had not given thought.
When our ship died, and from the broken deck,
I plunged 'mid moving mountains of the angered deep,
A slip of wild sea tangle looped 'round my heel.
Then had I not cast sandals from my feet,
I would have gone those paths where Hermes guides.
But what I loosed in desperate need, will bind me here,
For if I try my steps upon this shale,
I will be lame of foot by nightfall.

Old Man: Think not on this impediment.

Polysemous: How so?

Old Man: I make some thrift out of the dregs of loss.
You made of me a gift, now I to you.

[He presents him with a worn pair of sandals.]

Telegonos: My thanks. I am within your debt.

Polysemous: And now—

Telegonos: But mark you there, Polysemous, the rainbow?

Polysemous: I cannot see it. Where?

Telegonos: Have you not eyes?
Just there, it shimmers like a dream, to left
The fragment of that insubstantial moon.

Polysemous: I say again, I see it not.

Telegonos: It's gone.

Polysemous: And yet this augurs of our good.

Telegonos: Perhaps.

Polysemous: Let's go in haste.

Old Man: I'll with you, boy.

Xanthicus: This way.

[Exit severally. Telegonos remains on stage alone.]

Telegonos: Too well I now remember all his words,
That seer, that prophetman, who spoke to me
When we lay in at port of Naragon,
And plucked me by my sleeve, what time I lagged
Behind the rest, intent on my own thought,
And hailed me by my name, though never known.
You will, he said, your father's land have found,
When Iris' sign appears beside the fading moon,
Then vanished in the press. Yet what will answer such
But this I glimpsed above the dawning sea?

Oh, that I might have testament more sure!
Perhaps this is but fabric of my fantasy.
For since the wreck of all our fortunes,
I've waked and dreamed and waked again in terror,
Until I cannot sift the dreaming out the real.

What was it then?
That vision last, that roused me trembling?
I was transformed into a stock of wood,
That blindly tossed insensate on the sea,
But when I sought to strike against the tide,
Sank down, a stone, into the cold abyss.

[He raises his spear to the heavens.]

Oh savage ones who watch our fates from high Olympus,
Or if there lives some other god unknown to me,
Grant grace to me to find my father's isle,
And that some worthy interventor hand
Might bind in one strong bond the heavens and the earth!

Polysemous: *[From off stage.]* Come, Telegonos,
        and let's grasp up the day.

Telegonos: I'll after now, and make no more delay.

[Exit.]

ACT II

Same scene, midmorning.

[Enter Polysemous and Telegonos, above.]

Polysemous: You are angry.

Telegonos: Not so.

Polysemous: I say again you are.

Telegonos: Then so say, and so believe, and leave off
Saying until the very end of time!
My good Polysemous, you deem yourself
To be a sage and weighty counsellor,
In whom I should repose such trust I have.
Is it not so?

Polysemous: Many times upon our
Voyage have you sought me out among the rest,
To give advice on this or that small thing.

Telegonos: Then let me lay, front of the tempered edge
Of your keen cutting mind, a deadly foe
To all my understanding, that you may fell
With one sharp thrust.

Polysemous: In all, I am but yours.

Telegonos: I am but lately come to coast this
Jagged land unknown, and that, so wanting low
I walk its broken shores in borrowed shoes.
And in such poverty, I chanced across
A milk-white stag that hurtled through the brake
To nimble overleap a tumbled stump
And cantered slow to stop among the trees.
He looked a buck was fatted to the rut,
And I some motion made to cast my spear,
But of a sudden moment strange, my friend,
The ally and advisor to my cause,
Cries out and dashes arm against my arm,
Then calls out, "Fly!" as though he wished to save

The beast from any harm. Which same startled, shied,
And quick was lost within the dappling groves.
Now tell me, you who know so vast a store,
What should I think of one thus rash and wild?
Is he a madman or a fool?

Polysemous: There was
And is a reason in my act, although
In your vehement strain you know it not.

Telegonos: Then spindle me another cloth of words
To trick out your intent, or this you call
My strain may rend the fabric of the matter
And wrench it to a thousand mendless shreds.

Polysemous: You know, my Prince, that I cannot—

Telegonos: Why so?

Polysemous: I'm not a man who jibs his tongue to easy sail
Across a sea of words with turning wind
Of every new occasion but must have
Some star of thought by which to guide my way.
To sum the whole, your men yet live.

Telegonos: They live?
How know you this?

Polysemous: I had it from the boy,
Who saw them in the wood of yesternight.

Telegonos: They live? Why did you not speak on this before?

Polysemous: I did not dare to venture it in
Hearing of that old man, who has enforced on us
His presence and his person and his will.
Craftsome, cunning, and malign of influence
He seems to me. I do not trust him more
Than would I promise of a siren wild.
Some secret hides behind his shambled look,
And too unwinking is his eye.

TELEGONOS, ACT II

Telegonos: And yet,
He has his friendship proved with gift of these.
Of what condition are those friends we lost?
And what has this to do with your mad act?

Polysemous: Are you prepared to hear?

Telegonos: I am. Say on.

Polysemous: One night before we sailed, as I lay deep
In sleep beside our ship, one of the four
Who tend your mother's will laid hand on me,
And, when I had awakened, bade me rise.
Silent as a dream, we slipped out the camp
And mounted up the bluff, seen only by the waning moon.
No word she spoke as we two made our way
Beneath that hawk-wing gate and through the groves
To that great, towered house of dressed, bright stone.
But when among those columns red as vines in times
They wither, whispered she so low I scarce could hear,
"Be wise in word and act, oh man, and fear.
The anger of the savage gods is no light load
For mortal men to bear." Then guided she
My way through that vast, gilded banquet hall
Where feasts are held which have the power to make
A beast of any man. And on she led
Through passages whose walls with magic art
May speak and answer with a human sound
Until at last we came into a wide
And sulfur colored chamber deep within
Where Circe sat upon a pennoned throne
Of wood and mountain gold. I saw no lamp,
Yet blazed the room, as if it had been noon.

Telegonos: Such radiance the gods have at their beck.
My heart forebodes at this. But yet, resume.

Polysemous: Longwhile the goddess kept her still but held
Me with a speaking glance, then soft she said,
"Are you a man who can conceal what thing you know?"
I answered that I was. "You have," said she

"But spoken truth, for when I gazing make
Into men's eyes, I can discern their hearts.
I have a task for you that you must seal within."
Then she clapped twice, and through the arch of stone
Came one of those monstrous creatures wild that are
Not man or beast but walk the crooked earth
On ill-assorted limbs. This one gave to me
A sealed amphora jar, as if for wine.
Whence low her words came to my listening ear,
"But drip this lightly, drop by little drop,
On the tack within their hold, and all that feed
Thereon will so remain the man he is.
But should three days go by without its taste,
They will revert back to their beastish form.
But feast yourself and my own son on other food."
Then in great voice she cried aloud to me,
"Ward well the young man's life, I charge you here!
I, a goddess am, and so immune to all
That flesh and blood on earth inherit.
Not so, Telegonos my son and only heir!
This journey's end I cannot see, nor scan
The tablet where men's fates are written down,
But something broods within my heart that grows
And knows I shall not see my son again!"
I assented to her will and soon came back
To where I was before. Your men yet live,
And yet they live no longer men, but range
At large the world in animal disguise.

Telegonos: Oh, grievous word!

Polysemous: Take not their fate so much to heart.

Telegonos: I have become a second Orpheus,
To gain and lose in but a single chance.

Polysemous: No, say not lose.

Telegonos: And yet, I have them not,
And they have not themselves. I know not who
To grieve the more. And you think that fair stag—

Polysemous: Not think, but know to be.

Telegonos: How so?

Polysemous: It wore
About its throat a pearlshell necklet string
That you have seen before.

Telegonos: Ah, Kalonous!
Too dear, the freedom that I bought for you!
For see how all things flow from us, dissolve,
And dwindle from our reaching and our grasp.
Yet loss will often spur to greater gains,
As fire that can consume but also forge.

Polysemous: But those who use the blade must know the hour
To thrust, and too, the time to ward the blow.

Telegonos: You are too cryptic, for I do not take your drift.

Polysemous: My prince, you are to fault an honest man.

Telegonos: Never have I counted such a failing.

Polysemous: I meant not that, but this is to the point.

Telegonos: Grind to finer sharpness then your meaning.

Polysemous: Candor's fruit is not always in season.

Telegonos: But falsehood leaves a foul and bitter tang
Within my mouth and is not to my taste.

Polysemous: And yet the sweetest taste is not of truth,
But wine of victory, that drink of kings.
For what is truth but something to be used?
As you have said, we've come to lands unknown
Where likely reigns a despot lord, whose whims
We cannot see. Yet you would open up
The port of all your plans to any ship.

Telegonos: You speak again on that old man?

Polysemous: The same.
To be so trustable to all's not wise.

Telegonos: Are you now a one to speak of whom to trust?
You are a faulty bow that shoots not straight!
How cursed that fatal hour should be when I
First took you to my closest confidence!

Polysemous: And yet I am no traitor to your cause,
Though you would reckon me to be such one.
I feared the dreadful mana of a goddess' word,
But while in part I have deceived, I never played you false.

Telegonos: Oh, would I might discern the springs of your intent!
But set that by for now. I don't forget
The service that you've rendered in the past.
Redeem this fault with usefulness, and I,
In time, will give reward.

Polysemous: But that which you
Call weakness, I well number as a strength.
And this is it that I would have you see.
This wide and patterned world is nothing but
A gaming board. To have first move can prove
A great advantage if it's used with skill.

Telegonos: What is it that you would have me do?

Polysemous: Add circumspection to the virtues you possess
And you shall be invincible.
So must you write out your intent as though
In cypher script and be in act obscure
And formless as the night, then watch your chance,
Cry victory, and claim the spoils of war!

Telegonos: Such knots you tie I left behind when I
Took leave my mother's isle.

Polysemous: Then recollect

The father that you seek, and consider
The horse of his design that conquered Troy.
For he is cunning, of many twists and turns,
And he would now approve of my advice.

Telegonos: There may well be some merit in this thought,
But in another hour I'll think on it,
For now I have remembrance in my mind.
A little knowledge I possess of that bad art,
By which my mother lashes 'round with cords
Of slavish bondage all the race of men.
There is a golden flower some call haemony,
The which if brewed for length of time can cure
The malady that ails our men.

Polysemous: Would that
Such simple could now avail us.

Telegonos: It may yet.
Within the orchard vale where jumped the buck,
I glimpsed a slope was dashed with yellow blooms.

Polysemous: You think they are that herb you said just now?

Telegonos: It may prove so. Let's hasten now and see.

Polysemous: I'll with you in a moment's slip of time.

[Exit Telegonos.]

Polysemous: Now springs to hand a chance by which may I
Make good my vow to her. For this, my prince,
Is of an overchildlike cast of mind,
And much unseasoned in the ways of all the earth.
Note well, how lies the shadow of this king
Across the folds and thrustings of his country.
If I may dare believe the boy, here hangs a fruit,
So heavy, ripe, and lavish to the hand,
The one who would refrain must count himself a fool.
When soon by art our crew has been restored,
We will have strength to match this warlike cause,

And, though we be but fifty men in all,
Such fifty, if they stood against the king,
Could rouse a disaffected multitude.

But I must school Telegonos, my prince,
In such hard acts as those will win it,
And justly govern him who governs me,
That he may with a step mount up this island's throne,
And leave aside this overbold attempt
To find that Ithaca wherein his father dwells.
For if he will ascend, so too shall I,
And have like state to what I was before.

Telegonos: *[From offstage.]* Ho there, Polysemous, be swift of foot!

Polysemous: I'll follow now, that I may lead in other after days.

[Exit Polysemous.]

[Enter Caissa and Diotima from right above.]

Diotima: I cannot answer. I scarce can say he loves me.
Though he be taking as Narcissus,
I fear I have become like Echo to this tale.
When we are two amid a company,
He shuns to give me word or kindly glance,
Or if I have contrived more private speech,
He strives a bluff and teasing part to play.

Caissa: Yet still.

Diotima: Oh, do not say, 'yet still,' in such a tone.

Caissa: Yet still.

Diotima: Oh, very well, and have your say.

Caissa: I judge the case, that he is something over shy,
And should you now lay siege with winning looks and smiles,
Be delicate the more that he is rough,
When he is cold as stone be warm as living fire,

You may then find his heart a citadel
That's easy overthrown. But now, enough!
What will you wear to round the coming festival?

Diotima: I had not given thought to such. My heart—

Caissa: Your heart would be much better served
To lose an hour or two in merriment,
For love is sweet, but life is sweeter yet by far.
Come now, I have a gown I'll lend you out
Of deepest jet that's spangled with a lace of ivory,
While I shall go in gold and summer blue,
Then we can dance together as the day and night.

[Enter Calidus and Callimachus from left.]

Calidus: Caissa! Ho there! Well met, on this bright morn!
Where are you bound? To tend your flock, I'll warrant.
What pleasure is to see such beauty in the wilderness!
And shall you now acquaint me to your friend?
She looks in lonesome sort, and I would but console her.

Caissa: Be done such idle talk. Her heart is most
Bespoke already. Pay him no heed.
He always prattles thus. And you, oh Calidus,
The son of Kalander, what errand brings
Your feet so far from paths where commonly they tread?

Callimachus: Our lord, the king Odysseus, himself,
Has charged us with a certain business in this place.

Caissa: There seems but little in these margins here
To suit the talents you possess, Callimachus.
Perhaps you've come to poll the loyalty
Of trees and herbs and flowers of the field?

Diotima: I've heard the peonies may be inclined
To practice some revolt against the state,
And, too, there's been some talk among the daffodils.

Callimachus: It is a secret thing that we may not give out.

Caissa: May not give out? But why? Oh, what a weight
To bear such solemn and so serious a charge!
I must, in truth, now tell of this to all
The maids who dwell within the village close,
For they would have it so, that you are but
A wantwit sort, but I must now chastise
Against their too, too merry and rebellious tongues.

Callimachus: I think you mock.

Caissa: Oh, never would I mock
A man so grave and so severe as you.

Calidus: Come now, Callimachus, our task is not
So secret as to prevent it from the eyes
Of friends. In short, we've come behalf a dream,
A woman, and a riddle of a stone.

Caissa: Lord Calidus, I think I must be fairly played on
And have return for all my jibing words.

Calidus: No, no. Say out, Callimachus. Do I
Not speak the truth?

Callimachus: Ask me not more,
For I will be as silent as the grave.

Caissa: Oh, would to gods it might be so hereafter.
Now who the woman tell, and whose the dream?

Calidus: It is the noble dreaming of the king,
Odysseus our lord, that sends us here
To scurret back and forth like mice chased by
A stooping hawk. Remember you the storm
Passed some days back?

Caissa: Would I could forget.
It wrought such damage to my holding pens,
I've scarcely finished up the mending.
But come regale me with the story's fullness now.

Calidus: Strange rumor, I suppose, crept in our sovereign's ear
Of some black ship wrecked on our island coast that night.
And while he mused distracted on this theme,
He fell into a dream, wherein he wandered
Empty passages his house alone,
Seeking something he could never name.
Then there appeared a wonder to his sight.
Although he felt no hint of stirring wind,
A single feather, colored like the sky,
Slid on the air and drifted down the hall.
Amazed, the king pursued and traced its path
To come before an unremembered door,
And drawing back the bolt he entered in.

He found an altar chamber there, illumined by
A pure and radiant darkness that filled his heart
With peaceful terror and with a dread delight.
Through vantage of a window wide, he glimpsed
A wheel of icebright stars against the night.
Of sudden, he perceived a maiden fair,
Clothed with a soft candescence of the sun,
Who spoke in accents of the sounding sea.
"All hail, Odysseus, who sacked the city Troy."
And he, "All hail, great queen," but he knew not her name.
Then she, as though divining all that lay
Within his troubled mind, said forth, like song,
"I am The Lady Called-Out-From-Among.
 See you this stone?" And looking where she indexed with
Her eye, he found an ancient massy block,
All over carved with runes and symbols dark.
"You now behold," she said, "The head that joins the corner.
Countless are they will fall, and too
Shall many rise, because this stone was hewn.
He that falls on it shall mercy gain,
But him on whom it falls, shall there be pashed
In piecings small." Then welled the anger of
Odysseus and he said hot, "And what
Have I to do with this offensive stone?"
"Much and yet but little," she replied.
"All things that are, are in division three.
Three nights gone by, there wrecked a ship on these

Your island coasts. Seek out its crew. The rock
Commands you to this labor and this cause,
For this event concerns your very life.
Only to its captain, will you reveal
Yours and this island's name." Then summoned she
The four that guard the hinges of the winds,
Which guide men right when on the sea they fare.
They handed him a scroll sealed with a triple seal,
Impressed with form of creatures three. They seemed
An owl for love, a milk white hind for good
Belief, and then the Phoenix bird that in
A wondrous year arises from the flame.
And so abashed, our lord cried out to know
The meaning of the roll. And she to him
"It is the letter written by the stone,
Which you will yield alone to him that watches on
The vessel's fate. And now farewell," and she
Clapped thrice 'til all the room filled up with noise
Of roaring wind.

When he awaked and knew
It for a dream, he straightly he sent for us,
To bid us range the edges of the land
In this wild and fairy chase. Is it not
The very cream of mirthful jest that we
Now smire through all these meadows green upon
The substance of a dream?

Caissa: Yet often is
Our dreams unwind some movement of the times
Or show in shifting figures shifting sense
That lead us light-winged to the truth.

Calidus: Oh, come; it is a piffling thing, as weighty as
The spindrift foam that's born on ocean currents.

Callimachus: Or else a lie sent not through gates of horn.

Caissa: I cannot say. It may in time prove so.
But look below. Some remnants of a fire
Are dying on the beach. Perhaps you have now found

Your master's fancy from the land of Nod.

Callimachus: Let's down and see, and well remember this,
We must not name the king or Ithaca.

Calidus: The part we play is clear. Ho, onward, feet, and move.
So fare you well, Caissa sweet, and you, fair maid.

Caissa: Perhaps I'll see you at the festival. Farewell.

[Exit all.]

[Enter Telegonos, Polysemous, the Old Man, and Xanthicus, severally below.]

Telegonos: My thanks to both of you, for you have gathered in
A goodly portion. Stoke up the blaze
And fill the cauldron at that springhead there,
For we have much that needs to stew awhile.

Xanthicus: And what are we to cook?

Telegonos: But these.

Old Man: You are
But starking mad, oh Prince, or else you lark,
For no man solid in his reason's power
Fed yet the corners of his mouth on such
Like flower feast. But be ensured on this
The climbing sun has burnt you in your brain.

Telegonos: I am not mad, but in a merry sort of mind.
For know you well that by these petals gold
Our fortunes may rise up. What sound is that?

[Enter Callimachus and Calidus.]

Calidus: Hail, strangers! We give you greetings of the morning!
Most surprised are we to find you in this place,
And judge you may be foreign to these shores.

Polysemous: It is a fair beginning, but I fear the end.

Telegonos: Soldiers, you have our thanks. You are correct
In thinking us to be but newly come
Within your bounds. In truth, we are even
As is a very night of ignorance
And know not where we are.

Callimachus: Who are you men,
That shelter in this cove so desolate,
And what that country your fathers call as home?

Polysemous: We are of Crete and bred of noble stock.
Our ship was ravaged on the sea by low
And filthy brigandmen. We four devised
Escape, and now await our kinsmen.

Calidus: Then know you naught of some proud galley
That lately broke upon these promontories?

Polysemous: Nothing, save these scattered signs
That bear mute testament to such a loss.

Calidus: You see? Have I not said it from the first?
We but lose time that cannot be regained.

Callimachus: But we best hale this lot before the king
To show our toil.

Calidus: Most noble sirs, our lord the king
Would doubtless be distressed at your misfortunes.
How then, shall we not bid you to his halls?

Polysemous: Our present state is not so ill a thing.

Telegonos: And what the name of your good king that we
Should give him thanks? Come, sirs, be not silent.
It is a simple matter I request.

Calidus: Such questions will their answers find within
Our city walls. But follow now and be our guests.

Telegonos: How is called this island and your town?

TELEGONOS, ACT II

Calidus: Account of these you'll have but later on.

Telegonos: Yet askings I have now. If you intend
No subterfuge, I charge you speak it plainly.

Calidus: What plainer sense than this, we bid you come.

Telegonos: Why will you not say what is your sovereign's name?

Calidus: It is an elder custom of this land.

Telegonos: A custom strange, to muffle so a name.

Calidus: Will you not come? It would be better so.

Telegonos: On one condition will I go with you.
Tell to me your ruler's name and what this kingdom is.
This I earnestly entreat you by the gods!

Calidus: You ask of me a thing I cannot do.

Callimachus: Beware the hospitality of kings to scorn!

Polysemous: How quick he goes from coax to menacement.

Calidus: We threaten not, but only warn. Heed us.
Come now, and give attention to my words.

Telegonos: Your words? Too well have I heard all your words.
You bid us come, and yet will tell not where,
And urge us to be guested by a king who is
By custom never named. We are not fools!
An honest man would answer with the truth.

Calidus: But rightly think on this, Oh, man of Crete,
Receipt of gifts is honor to the one who gives.
Just so, rejection is a shame to him.
Why bring dishonor to our sovereign lord?

Callimachus: He who shames king, exalted as we serve
Stands in much peril, and will most shortly suffer it

And forfeit up his life with deadly pain.

Polysemous: Now he speaks plainly! How ugly is
The monstrous face we common glimpse behind
The state's too smiling mask.

Telegonos: Enough! Servants, hear me speak!
These warlike postures daunt me none the least.
Look well upon this spear and know that death
Awaits my foes on its envenomed point.
We are well able to defend ourselves.

Polysemous: And it may be we're not so reft of brave
Companions as we now appear. You've given us
Your warnings, now we give back to you.

Callimachus: Were it not for honor to my lord king
I'd answer all your words with bitter deeds.
But we will go now to our sovereign's house
To make report. I think in aftertime,
You will long rue your speeches of this day.

Calidus: I hesitate to leave the matter thus,
But seems it best we may depart. So shall we go.

[Exit Calidus and Callimachus.]

Polysemous: Let me pass by. Why do you stare?

Old Man: The first, were you
A fishingman, next servant to a prince
Shipwrecked upon these ragged rocks,
And now have you become a lord of Crete
Escaped but late from pirate hands, and I
Await what further transformation should occur.
Perhaps now like a phoenix bird you'll molt
In flame of fire and fly into the reaches of air.

Polysemous: A tactic, sir, a trick and nothing more.
It gains for us a space of time to breathe.

Telegonos: And yet I wish you had not done so,
For lies cling to the skin of those who wear
Their aching shape like that tormenting cloak
Fair Deianera gave. A pretty game
Of nine men's morris now we play with them.
But come here, boy, and lug it to the fire.

Polysemous: When that is done, we will collect our friends
And so untwist for them the knot that Circe tied.
Perhaps this day will see us march against
The citadel and storm the presence of
This wicked, nameless king. I think that such a deed
Befits the son of wise Odysseus,
Who with his cunning arts sacked city Troy.

Telegonos: Be done with that. I want no war with him.

Polysemous: You err in this, my Prince. We must strike first.

Telegonos: If it shall come to that, then it shall come.
But I am troubled in my mind about this king
We must have knowledge sure that he intends us ill.

Polysemous: What surer proof do you require my lord
Than what those messengers have said of late?

Telegonos: I have another reason in my thought.

Polysemous: Even to a mind untutored in
That art of politics, it must appear
As written large how great is the disease
Of tyranny which so infects this state.

Telegonos: By your design we are now solitary.
What is it you would say to me? Speak it.

Polysemous: Take but a moment then to raise your eyes.
Glance down the mistfar reaches of this island coast;
See how its rocks give way to greenery.
It is a rugged land, but rich in soil.
If but its government were just, it could

In splendor rival sandy Pylos.

Telegonos: You think by such an argument to sway
Me from my chosen course.

Polysemous: I only wish you take
Consideration with a reasoned mind.
What hopes we all once had that we might reach
That Ithaca in which your father rules
Are now but faint. But here about us lies
A kingdom ready-made, which if we 'bide
The proper moment we may conquer.

Telegonos: Enough! I will not listen further.
I did not drive to sea for such as this.
I seek Odysseus, my father!

Polysemous: But why, Oh prince? Must it be only so?
Many kingdoms are as great as Ithaca.

Telegonos: What other kindred do I have on this wide earth?
For I have broke with that immortal one who brought me forth.
For though a scion there of privilege,
Her shifts and cruelty I could no longer bear.
I have no place that I may call my own.
So I will seek my father on the restless seas
That I may know, at last, the one who made me,
And learn from him what is to be a mortal man.
How often I have imaged in my mind
That moment first when we shall meet and have
Some tender recompense for all my years of pain.
But leave these words until another time;
The sun is hot, and I feel need of sleep.
Perhaps my former illness now returns.

Polysemous: I too am strangely wearied by the heat.

Old Man: Then sit you down and rest from all your labors,
For patience is that noble art
Which makes us most like to divinity.

[They sleep.]

ACT III

TELEGONOS, ACT III

Same scene, noon.

[Enter Odysseus, above, disguised as a peddler. He wears an eyepatch.]

Odysseus: How secret is the journey I have made!
When I trucked by the slates and gables of the town,
None dreamed Odysseus their lord passed by,
But took me for the shabby peddler which I seemed.
Now I am botched with dust and true must look the part,
That should I glimpse a viewing glass I'd laugh to see it.
But that prophetic vision of the night
Eats at my mind, devours all peace like cancer.
This point concerns your very life, she said;
The dreamstone has commanded you this charge.
Then still, while I sat trembled with this cause,
My servants give account of one who shakes
A proud barbaric spear and hints a force may march
Up to the strong built gates of clear seen Ithaca!
They must imagine it an easy matter
To conquer one who reigns and steal his land!
Hard will they find it though, for I am hard.
But halt, speech. This region is familiar.
Ha! By the gods, shall I not say this is the very reach,
Now twenty years gone by, where I returned
And hid my treasures got from the hand of Alcinous?
But halt again. Hush! Caution! What stirs below?
Why is but a poor quartet of sleeping men!
I have my bow. How if proud palest death
Should take them from these heights while they
Lie muffled snug within the arms of Morpheus?
But, no. I hinder on this thought. They would
Not sleep so sound, unless a watch were kept.
I will beguile their minds until I learn their strength
And wind them in a labyrinth of my lies.
Hence now, Odysseus, until the time's more fully come
That you might play them most to your advantage.

[Exit.]

[Telegonos awakens.]

Telegonos: What? Dare we now to dream? Rise up!
The eyes of the island may be watching.
Awake! See how has climbed the light, while we
Have cast away the morn within the Sandman's halls.

Polysemous: Three grains of rice and the working of a bird's wing.
Your pardon, noble Prince, I fear I dreamed.

Telegonos: I too, but fitfully, and none the softest stuff,
For I became a second Actaeon
Set on by my own hounds and mangled.
It is not fit to keep so lax a guard when we
Have those who make themselves our adversaries.

Old Man: Be easier in heart, oh Prince, it is more fit.

Telegonos: No, I do not love to wait and would not now be idle.

Old Man: Yet what you brew within that vessel there
Whiffs to my nose a little underdone.
And even gods, my lord, will sometime take their ease
To rest from motions of the world at large.
What harm if we may follow suit?

Telegonos: Rest is but vain tedium to me,
And we are set at odds against the king.
We must by some necessity breathe here a time
But use it well and still be watchful.
How stirs the broth?

Xanthicus: I cannot say. Come and see.

Old Man: A moody, pettish kind of prince.

Polysemous: True that.

Old Man: What have you there?

Polysemous: A gaming board of sorts. I found
It buried in the sand, hard by my head, when I awoke.

Old Man: Perhaps some flotsam of your vessel's end?

Polysemous: None of our crew could boast so rich a gift,
And by its battered time-scarred cast, I'd say
It has lain there through many spinning years.

Old Man: Take back the lid and let us see within.
Although its outward part is full of harm,
Within it looks as when new made.
It is the pastime men call tau.

Polysemous: You know it then?

Old Man: I've played its like in days gone by.

Polysemous: Instruct me then, and let us fill the void
That broods about this waiting hour. I ever was
A master at such strokes.

Old Man: Boast not until
You've won the round. But still I'll have a turn with you.

Telegonos: It's looking well. A thing in earnest I
Would sound you on while we two are apart.
Do you remember when we earlier dispersed?

Xanthicus: I do.

Telegonos: Did you not see the rainbow as it clung
Close by to shoulder of Hyperion's
White daughter, Moon, which dreamed above the sea?

Xanthicus: I well recall how you remarked it,
But I was much distracted on another thought my own,
And so I traced it not. What does it matter?

Telegonos: If you will keep this theme in confidence
I will relate it in a word or two.

Xanthicus: You have my silence.

Telegonos: And you, my trust.
Once in a port we kept along our way
I met a man who made his bread by augury.
A prophecy he spoke to me that I would find
The kingdom of the father that I seek
When I had seen a rainbow by the moon.
But now this speech is constant in my mind,
And hosts of fears make war against my hope.

Xanthicus: Oh, sir, it cannot be. This land is evil,
This kingdom's lord a wicked murderer.
They say he is ingenious as a rook
But honors not the customs or the laws of men.
Come; give no heed to signs of wheeling birds,
Nor tongues of those who would divine for gold,
But trust now on the instinct of your heart.

Telegonos: Perhaps you say this well. Perhaps you're right.

Old Man: Scatter out the chancing sticks upon this stone.

Polysemous: Ha ha! A four! My hounds are fleet of foot!

Old Man: Now I, in turn. Look how my lion leaps ahead!

Polysemous: Don't dare to roar so loud, old man, you've yet to win.

Xanthicus: Now I would ask a thing of you, and one
More cheerful to this waiting hour.
Truly as it seems you've travelled far to find
Your father's shore. All of your lore and ways
Are foreign to my island mind. Come, tell to me
The tale of all your restless outward goings,
For I would have some knowledge of the lands beyond.

Telegonos: Well spoke! Such words reveal a noble mind,
For understanding is the food of souls,
And truth a glad communion to our hearts.

Xanthicus: Then set before me such a banquet now.

TELEGONOS, ACT III

Telegonos: Know first, that with a double purpose
I made this voyage upon the iron sea.
For all men know the deep malicious hate
My goddess mother holds for all the race of mortal kind,
And in the springs of my intent lay this,
To find my father's land, and at one stroke,
To rescue certain of her captive host.

When safely we embarked from Circe's island,
Some shores we touched where lived a simple folk,
Who wove but tapa cloth and marked their skins with signs,
And other whiles, we were of nights received
Like royal guests in palaces of kings.

But though we did inquire most earnestly
None might show the course my father's city lay,
That city whose builder and maker is the
Great king, in which like and image I am craft.
But when we lay enharbored in that citadel
Amana, the one who kept our helm,
In sleepings of the night, rose up and journeyed in a dream.
He crossed the dark and violet seas
To stand, in but in a vision, upon the brink
Of some far eastern island country.
With corners three its bluffs and palisades
Rose up to meet the marching of the tide.
Then by a revelation and by a mystery,
He knew it for my father's land and knew the way to seek.

Polysemous: Aue! I've passed the gate. My luck holds firm.

Old Man: Beware! My lions prowl and hunger for the prey.

[Enter Calidus and Callimachus above.]

Calidus: Stop now, and tell it out to me in full.
What words are we to use when first we see him there?
Are we to rush from out these rocks with warlike shout?
Or is the scope of his devising other sort?

Callimachus: No, no, he enjoined on us no words but sense.

The king in imitation walks the land.

Calidus: In imitation, say? What is this strange
Disguise of speech? It does not suit your state.

Callimachus: Ha, yet is the suit that will disguise the state.

Calidus: Such is not an answer to my charge.
      Come, speak plain.

Callimachus: A costume, then. He wears a costume of one
Who hawks his wares within the public street,
And other than his own true self he seems.

Calidus: And to what end does he play out this masquerade?

Callimachus: To lure them, see. To bind their minds in cords
Against such hour their bodies may be bound.
And in the bluff of this too cheating fiction,
We also have a part to play.

Calidus: I take you now, and grows within my mind
Some wild surmise as what he wishes.

Callimachus: Attempt to tell the way of it. I will attend on you.

Calidus: Say then that we descend to these below
And offer up the same we did before.

Callimachus: So far your shafts strike well at what they aim.

Calidus: Next comes it that Odysseus, our king,
Makes entrance on the scene in garment like
A wandering peddler man, as you set forth.

Callimachus: Well said.

Calidus: It follows so, we make as if
He were a rogue, that by some fault of law
Is banished hence.

TELEGONOS, ACT III

Callimachus: Good, good.

Calidus: We will, in short,
Endeavor hard, as if in wrath to seize him.
But he, as being one pitiable
And abject in such cause, will make appeal,
Which suit the outlanders will take to heart.
When we have made a feint and feigned retreat,
The king will gather in their confidence,
And by some yet unfashioned ploy, will lead
Their steps on paths to where an ambush waits.

Callimachus: You speak as would the very oracle of truth!
Such was the sum of all that he conveyed.

Calidus: I know his mind, you see, at least in broad.

Old Man: One, two and three, and see your hound removed.

Polysemous: Have care, old man.
    A cur once kicked grows bitish mean.

Telegonos: We voyaged on into an unknown sea
And slipped so swift on through the waves, where sported
Dolphins in the green and silver surges,
It seemed the very deep gave loud acclaim
To all our charge. One evening, as the sun
Sank down in liquid fire and molten clouds
In color like the stone that men call jacinth,
One of our crew, who silent was most times,
Brought forth a polished lyre on which he played
And tuned his tongue to sing of kings long gone.
Whence rose up from the brine the people of the sea,
With countenance that 'sembled ancient bronze,
Who times would listen to his music,
Yet in some raft of notes would harmonize,
With weighty voice, a lay their own in language of the deep.

Calidus: But say what place did he appoint our ambush to?

Callimachus: Here I am blank, for we spoke not on this.

I hope it shall lie close to hand, for then
My sword will take just vengeance for their words.

Calidus: This bluster makes me think
You stopped at tavern on the way you came.

Callimachus: Not so, for on the eggs of owls I fed in youth,
A sovereign charm against the wiles of wine.

Calidus: We do not know the king intends their death.

Telegonos: Not more a sevenday ago, we lay
In harbor at the port of Rogaven,
Whose governor suspected us as spies
And cast in prison certain of our crew,
Until we took departure out his lands.
So bound by sad necessity, although the sky
By tokens and by signs forbade us sail,
We made on through immortal hours of night.

Old Man: The game will now at odd and even squares proceed.

Polysemous: Not so. I think you use some fiendish trick!

Old Man: You rate too low that skill which old men have.

Callimachus: Oh, far too well I know his mortal will,
For you caught not his glance. The eyes of kings
Speak volumes of the night in their disdain.
Though I am minded not to subtle doors,
And still prefer a straighter fight to this deceit.

Calidus: I think you have not long been so retained
In service to Odysseus, our lord.
Many are the turnings of his cunning.
He is the father too of lies. It is his mind
To win not honestly, when stealth may gain the day.

[Exit.]

Telegonos: The wind cried out as would the dead in agony

And moved all things that lay before its power,
Then fell the jagged lightning blast, so fierce,
As we whirled round like jetsam on the heaving deep,
Rove down our mast in instant to a cinderstump,
And spoke with sudden thunder, of so vast
A voice, it seemed not sound but sheerest force.
The night around was like a blind man's dream,
For sun, nor moon, nor any light of stars
Came to our eyes. No world we had. No world,
Save only pelting rain and ceaseless noise and dark.

Xanthicus: And that the storm which drove your ship to wreck
Here on this many mountained land?

Telegonos: How's that?
Yes, just so. I crave your pardon, friend.
This memory lies hard across my heart.
These roots and herbs are now most neatly steeped.
Come close, Polysemous, and I will, by a word,
Instruct you in this remedy's good art.

Polysemous: It was a losing game at any odds,
But here I will swear oaths, you cheat. It's true.

Old Man: Such robadoes of fortune you must learn to bear.
The casting sticks lie not. But go and serve your master's will.

Polysemous: Another time I'll prove my skill with you.

Xanthicus: Why do you sniff the wind?

Old Man: It smells of death.

[Enter Calidus and Callimachus.]

Calidus: Oh, men of Crete, well met in happy hour!
Our king is clement and sends us yet again
To pledge good faith and hospitality.

Telegonos: And has your answer changed with passing time
That changes all for good or ill?

Calidus: What answer, sir?

Telegonos: Will you not now reveal what land is this
And who is monarch here?

Calidus: Oh, would I could.

Telegonos: Your words are as immutable as stones.

[Enter Odysseus, disguised as a peddler, singing and towing a wheeled cart.]

Odysseus: *Come 'round, come 'round,*
From stead and village farm and town!
A peddler with his cart of clay,
And sounding out a token bell,
Draws near you on his rambling way
With merchandise to sell!
So come now all and cast off your cares!
Come now all and buy of my wares!
Medicines, fabrics textured and fine,
Treasures and trinkets and jars of rare wine.
All things that are bought may also be sold.
So hearken my toll and hasten with speed.
Your jit or your win or your jangle of gold
May purchase you here what all you may need.
Come 'round, come 'round,
From stead and village farm and town!
A peddler with his cart of clay,
And sounding out his token bell,
Draws near you on his rambling way
With merchandise to sell!

Callimachus: You there, be shut that cant and clangor of your trade!

Odysseus: Oh, harshest fate that I have hithered here!

Calidus: Is it not him?

Callimachus: It is the very truth.

Calidus: Unless I am mistaken in my sight

You are that selfsame chapman that our lord,
Some fortnight by, made public proclamation,
To the effect that you are banished hence.

Odysseus: I'm not a man to shade the truth. I'll not deny it.

Callimachus: Say then how it comes thus, that you make bold
To cry your wares as if it were not so?

Odysseus: Good masters, you are but just.
Yet I am poor and wretched miserable and low,
And seek not from you merely what is just,
But rather crave your mercy and your kindness,
For there are other eyes than those of kings,
Who watch the world of men to mark how each
Fulfills the duty that he owes his brother.

Callimachus: Think not to play upon our sympathies,
For we have none.

Calidus: Nor will you by this trick of speech
Move us to an unfit reverence of the gods,
Who mark more truly how each fulfills the law.

Callimachus: Whose just command we will not falter to obey,
And bring you bound before the judgement seat.

Odysseus: *[To Telegonos.]* Have mercy, friend, I pray you here, be kind.

Telegonos: Cease you, servant, until you tell what crime
This one performed.

Callimachus: This instance is of no concern to you.

Polysemous: How if we yield him not?

Calidus: What cause have you to meddle so within
Affairs that soar beyond your scope and ken?

Telegonos: That justice which is due to every man
Is well within my power to know.

Callimachus: Stand aside there. We have no quarrel with you.

Odysseus: Around the seven seas all men are brothers, sir.
Have mercy now and save your fellow man!

Callimachus: Come hither you!

Polysemous: Stand back!

Calidus: Give way and let him go!

Odysseus: Help! Violence!

[They struggle.]

Telegonos: Go back now, soldiers, to your sovereign lord
Daunted by the terror that I hold,
For brave men still abide, who will not buckle to
The proud mouthed ravings of a tyrant king!

Callimachus: These blows and vaunting jibes
       have set you to your fate.
We go now to our king to take up this report.

[Exit.]

Odysseus: Good young master, you have my grateful praise.
It is an act more worthy of a god than of a man!

Telegonos: Be done such talk. I have now set myself
In enmity against the human king
Who rules these rugged lands, I would not court
The envy of immortal deities as well.

Odysseus: Peace, friend, be not so very angry.
I meant no ill. The fiery heat of quarrels rough
Will often fret the temper or swell a man
To say somewhat opposed to piety.
But I have stock in wagonload of vintage
That glads the heart and drives out bitter strife.
Such conflicts are a thirsty sort of work.

TELEGONOS, ACT III

Telegonos: It's good, for still my blood is burning.

Odysseus: *[Sings as he measures out the wine.]*

Though Sunday's hours be filled with light,
Moonday we will walk by night,
Starday dance upon the stair,
For Windsday brings a load of care.
On Thirstday may a man drink deep,
Fireday come he'll fall asleep.

Take this of me in token of my thanks,
And let this milder fire of wine cool down
The beat within your kindled veins. Rejoice now,
Then after share around the bowl to all our friends.

Polysemous: It has been long since honey-hearted wine
Has passed my teeth. It is well thought of.
But tell me, stranger, if you may, what cause
Has set you to this discord with the king.

Odysseus: Longwhile since by, I was a man of high degree
Who joined in fight to overthrow the king
Who holds the governance of nearby Samos.
Yet in this action we were prospered not at all.
So, I myself, gashed near to death with many wounds,
Fell captive to the adversary,
And thence was sold a slave upon the auction block.
When I, in after years regained such rights
As free men have, I took this tinker trade to win my bread.
And all went well, until of late, the king
Caught wind my name and knew my history,
Then from a pledged alliance to his neighbor state
Sought prudently to cast me out his bounds.
No, drink not first, young man, but pass the bowl
To him that overmatches you in age.

Old Man: I will not drink.

Polysemous: Oh, what an absurd old fool!
How ready you were but some slight sift of hours ago

To pester, prowl, and importune on us,
And then your chat was all of wine and flesh.

Old Man: This wine I will not drink.

Odysseus: Since I, though houseless here,
Am as host, I rule that none shall drink
Against their will. Young master, I would know a thing.

Telegonos: In that we are as one.

Odysseus: How's that? I do not take you.

Telegonos: I too have questions in my heart and mind,
But I'll forgo and set them by for now.
Ask what you will, I'll tell it if I know.

Odysseus: As I gave out, I played in youth a hero's part
And somewhat am acquainted the arts of arms,
Yet never have I seen in hands of mortal men
A spear that's fit to equal this you bear.

Telegonos: It was a gift of one who friends my house.

Odysseus: Although it is a weapon fine, it seems a thing
A deal too pretty for the bitter work of war.

Telegonos: Though it look delicate, it can well kill,
Be sure of that, and I have used it so.

Xanthicus: It is the craft of an undying hand.

Odysseus: The vengeful gods rarely give their gifts to men.

Telegonos: Within my veins there beats the blood of a
Dread goddess of the West. And this is grant
From out the hand of that lame smith who limps within
Olympus's golden halls.

Odysseus: I think you play,
In this, on that credulity that the old

Are thought to have.

Polysemous: Scoff not. He speaks the truth.

Odysseus: No, I will credit not such talk until
I hear the framing substance of the tale.

Telegonos: Then listen well to that which I relate.

Odysseus: Nothing so delights my heart as but
To hear a tale that's aptly told. Proceed.

Telegonos: In groves my goddess mother sacred keeps,
Once grew a vast hulupu tree, and she
Desired its timber rare to craft herself a throne.
Yet at its root there dwelt a monstrous serpent fierce,
Who fed on poisoned herbs and knew no charm.
This angered much the goddess, and she feared at it.
But then one springling day came questing one
Whose sire she had enslaved. Geos was his name,
A son to Kalonous, a nobleman of Thrace.
Hearing of this tale, he thought to trade
Against his father's life to kill the snake.
So Geos strode the green and meeting vales
Into the sacred groves and bravely fought for many hours
Against that beast. But when the sunlight shafted red
Into the forest glen, he grappled close
And with his blade found out its inmost heart.

The serpent dead, the goddess true her word
Released his captive sire and signalized
The glad event with feasts held in her halls.
I toasted him at this, and in our cups,
We two became fast friends. So when at last
They went the harbor mouth to take their ship for home,
I gladly walked beside them to the pier.
But only grief the fates had woven for that day.
For Geos, while he waded in the bay,
Not wary where he stepped, grazed on the back,
With searching foot of that dread ray, whose sting
Is in its poisoned tail. We heard his cry

And rushed to aid, but only came too late.
But as we held him there amid the heaving surf,
He gripped my arm, as spasm wracked his frame,
And thrust his knifehilt in my hand, to beg
Me take his vengeance on that devil of the deep.
Then with great love and anger in my heart,
I swashed through riling waves and swam out in the bay,
Out past the break to where the water cleared
And saw it there beneath. Longwhile I gave
It chase across the mirror of the sea.
How pale it looked and marked with cryptic signs.
Then when it dived, I took great draught of air
And too plunged down into the immense blue deep.
Drowned towers I saw there; the sheer of reef.
And I half blinded with the brine slow spiraled down
Toward where it unrushed glided, like a raptor 'mid
The twisting trees of stone that grew there on
The tawny ocean bed. A cloud of silver wrasse
Whirled 'round about my head as I too came
Inwith that forest mute, but when they cleared,
I spied my quarry close at hand, near where
Two seadales minglemet. It basked on silt,
Just next a silent plain, so stippled with
A thousand crimson bright anemones
It seemed a wildflower field that bloomed beneath
The shifting tide. Then taking up a piece
Of weighty plank I found there on a rock,
I pinned its sting and lunged, involved
In murk of roiling ocean drift and blood
Until I felt its roughness slack beneath my hand.
I took it up and fought with labored strokes
To rise to sun, to sound, and breathing wind.

The god Hephaistos came to our isle that night,
And marking on the bloody clothe about my head,
Took me aside and many questions made.
Then led me out beneath the spangled sky
And touched my trembling ear, and in brief time
We two flew up into the gusting dark.
All through the hours of the immortal night
We steered a course by bright Orion's stars

And by the Seven Sisters of the Sky,
But when the day broke clear among the island clouds
I saw a marvel on the brink of heaven deep,
A stony mountain cone, hung like a dream,
On nothing in the air. Then lighting on
The side of that vast alp we went within
To find the smithy that the god keeps there.
Wherein from secret veins and ingots of the cave
The god of fire forged this that you now see
And patterned it with warlike acts of mighty men.
See how it shines and catches back the light,
As if it were a mirror of my power.
But were that all, it still would be an instrument most deadly,
Yet by his subtle craft and greatest art
Hephaistos wrought into its furthest point
The venomed dart and poison of that ray.
That should my cast inflict a grazing wound
Its substance shall bring agony and death.

Odysseus: I am well satisfied, young master.
In days of youth I studied at my letters,
And is a pretty piece of rhetoric to be sure.

Telegonos: I am no courtier to fashion up a lie.
I spoke a very substance of the truth.

Odysseus: No doubt. No doubt. The world is marvelous.
But seems it to my mind you said of late you wished
To ask a thing of me.

Telegonos: I did. In truth, I did.
And one in which the debt of gratitude you owe
To our defense may fitly be repaid.

Odysseus: As much as lies with me in word or act
Or in intelligence, you'll have it.

Telegonos: Then say what name this island's sovereign wears.

Odysseus: I hesitate in speech on such a point.

Telegonos: No, speak! I urge, no, I command you speak!
You must. For we are brothered by his hate.
If fear imprisons so your tongue, know this,
That we are not as wanting in the help
Of friends to work our will. But only speak
And tell what now lies hidden in your heart.

Polysemous: My Prince, such words as these are not now wise.

Telegonos: Such cautious wisdom as you vend
I'll trade not for. It is enough. Be silent now.

Odysseus: You would his kingdom conquer then, it seems?

Telegonos: Yes seems! It is a world of seems, that I
Can never touch. A graspless world that slips
From me the more I hold it tight. And one
Name only in my heart I tremble lest you speak.

Odysseus: Aha. What name is that?

Telegonos: Odysseus.

Odysseus: How's this?

Polysemous: My prince, I fear your former illness has returned.

Odysseus: What word's escaped your teeth?

Xanthicus: It cannot be, good Prince.

Telegonos: I charge you here! Is it Odysseus
Who rules this land? Say out and speak the truth!

Odysseus: Odysseus?

Telegonos: Yes, such as that.

Polysemous: You see, he knows it not.

Telegonos: You're in the right. It cannot, must not be!

TELEGONOS, ACT III 73

Odysseus: Though this name and my own were one, I'd not
Have cause to tell you, even so. Nor can in truth
I now reveal this thing which you so eager seek.
For he who rules these shores, is shrouded in
Some mystery and wishes to remain unknown.

Telegonos: What's this?! Do none here on this blighted rock
Have knowledge of the one who governs them?
Savage gods! The world's a shifting dream.
None may awaken from it to a solid hour.
How violent and how vast this ocean mine!
It drowns me!

Odysseus: Come, come be peaceable, good prince,
And turn your thought to what can now avail us,
For this wild talk is but a tale of oak and stone.
The king has arms, has men, has plans, and time,
And what have you, but one fine spear and words?

Telegonos: What I have hinted darkly until now
I here, in faith and trust, make plain to you.
With many host of men I came to these
Too nighted shores. They will arrive here short.
Though poor in arms, they are yet rich in bravery.

Odysseus: So only weapons then are needed in your cause?

Telegonos: Just so.

Odysseus: I think I can repay in this,
The debt I owe to your defense.

Telegonos: Tell me.

Odysseus: Not more a stage from hence there lies a hut of stone.
It has been long abandoned many years,
But that dread majesty who rules these shores
Has used it as a cache against such times,
To hide therein some stock of armament.

Polysemous: And could you lead us to this place?

Odysseus: I can.
And more, can lead you to a secret breach
Within the city walls through which you may attack.

Telegonos: My thought of arms was only to defense.

Polysemous: Perhaps. But now is not a carefree hour.

Telegonos: You're for this course?

Polysemous: I am with all my heart!

Odysseus: How many men will need supply?

Polysemous: Some twice
Of twenty five, I think. Oh fearsome gods!
Do you not see, my Prince, the glory of
Such cunning ploy? We can defeat the king
On his own soil with spoil of his own arms.

Odysseus: And you, young man, would you not like to wear
The greaves and breastplate of a man of war?

Xanthicus: I do not know. I'm unaccustomed to the fight.

Odysseus: Said many a one the same before he felt
The heft of the hilt of sword within his hand.
Imagine what a hero's life must be!
Think how your kinsmen will revere you then.

Xanthicus: Such image as you paint within my mind
Now catches up my heart to restless fire!

Odysseus: That's spirit true! Will you not come, good sir?

Telegonos: I yet am hesitant to so provoke—

Odysseus: Good, Prince, for I perceive that you are good.
Are you not troubled with the niceties of war?

Telegonos: I do not say it so.

TELEGONOS, ACT III

Odysseus: Yet I will speak it for you.

Telegonos: I'm but in doubt on this.

Odysseus: Shall I not counsel you?

Telegonos: Speak it then, that I may judge the matter.

Odysseus: Would it not be the wiser and most prudent course
To cast aside the bars of your restraint?
Or do you think our common adversary
Would be as merciful and just to you?
You must now lay aside those golden dreams
Which sages and philosophers have dreamed,
Lest you shall find by some calamity
The world is not as they in their imaginations say.
How often are the good, in their pursuit
Of virtue, brought to nothing, brought to shame,
By cunning and by the craft of evil men.
You must then teach a little badness to your heart,
And learn how different evil is from good.

Polysemous: In truth, how many times have I not spoke the same?
It is desirable to be thus wise.
Have you not heard, Oh Prince, within our reach
This hazard comes to hand? Comes to our very hand!
Poor players we would be not to take such venture.

Telegonos: Silence! Leave off!
Speeches! Words! Chaos! I am engulfed!
Why should I sit and make attempt to calculate
The fittest course? For I was born a prince
And kindred to immortal gods!
Cringing at a prophet's word is not the part
My nature set me play, nor will I linger longer
In the shadow that this tyrant casts!
If this be doom it is a doom my own
To which I gladly go. Rise up! Prepare!

Polysemous: Oh, this is how I love you best, my Prince
And will yet serve you through a thousand battles.

No backward glance, then. Come, let us hasten.

Odysseus: I must a moment tend my wagon here.
Start up and I will after show the path.

Telegonos: My course is fixed. Be pleased to make no long delay.

[Exit all save Odysseus. Enter Calidus and Callimachus.]

Odysseus: You've heard the whole?

Callimachus: We have.

Odysseus: Good then.
Go now and make our preparations sure
To take them at the swineherd's lonely hut,
While I will lead their feet on paths not straight,
And at the Rock of Corax station one
That he may run and warn of our approach.

Callimachus: In this, we will obey.

Calidus: Now fare you well.

[Exit.]

Odysseus: See how this youth, who styles himself a prince,
Ascends and urges on that one who lags behind.
Such I was once, when on Parnassus' slopes
I hunted in my prime the scuffling boar.
How like a swiftlet on the wing my thought
Darts back to dip and pivot on the past.
Another man I was, another man,
With virtues many as the betony,
But how like this too foolish prince that hastes.
Yet here's a mystery, if ever was.
He fears, but still he seeks Odysseus!
Why? I see no cowardice in his glance.
This riddle I will soon unwind, oh Prince.
For when you've come within that shanty once
In times of old the good Eumaeus built,

TELEGONOS, ACT III

Many revelations will you make to me,
Oh, you, who claim descent from unknown gods.
But what is this that lies here on the face of rock?
A gaming board with pieces set to play.
It seems familiar to my touch and could well be
Some part that treasury from over sea I brought.
Think not, Oh Prince, Oh scion of the gods,
That I have come so far to only see
My kingdom overthrown by such you are.
No, no, the suffering and the agony
Of my return have taught into my heart
A lesson of no pity, but one of bitter hate
Lie there times past!
A game of other kind I am now set to play.
You seek Odysseus? You have him found!
On rocks your vessel suffered shipwreck then,
Now other sort this vortex you descend,
To there outface a dragon in his den!

[Exit.]

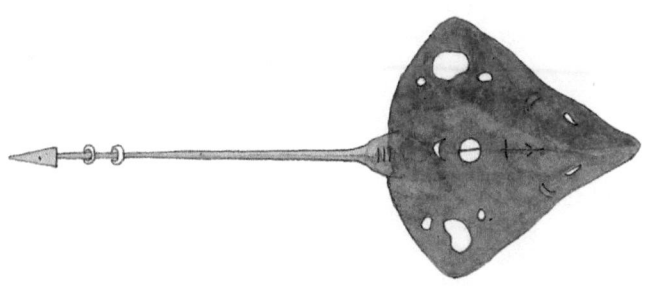

ACT IV

Same scene, late afternoon.

[Enter Polysemous and Xanthicus above.]

Polysemous: Not straight again!

Xanthicus: How's that you said?

Polysemous: Once more
These many paths have ranged our steps not right.
See, from our ledge and vantage on this bluff that cove
We sheltered at? But how may we descend?

Xanthicus: I cannot rightly see the way of it.
Some veer or cutting of the ragged track we've missed.
But stay; do you not hear behind that keening wail?

Polysemous: It is the wind; or else a falcon in
His crying gyre goes hunting on the air.

Xanthicus: It's ceased. And yet it held a human sound.

Polysemous: Nonsense.

Xanthicus: It was the voice of one in agony of pain.

Polysemous: A breeze from off the sea but frets
About this ruck of troubled stones and nothing more.

Xanthicus: Lend ear, it now returns. It's drawing close.

Polysemous: Be done such talk; it is the wind, I say!
Some subtle fear deceives and tricks your sense.

Xanthicus: I do not fear, but still my heart forebodes at it.

Polysemous: No, well could I perceive how when the prince
Sent we two back how changed and pale you grew.

Xanthicus: I do not fear.

Polysemous: It is no shame to own it.
But look now out and mark how brims the seaface.
With tides of light before the falling sun.
Such sights as these put courage in the soul.
In little time we shall have means of conquest.
Our victory is all but most assured.

Xanthicus: Just there, hard by that stand of tamarisk,
I glimpse a track that bends down to our place.

Polysemous: Well done. A lynx has not a sharper sight.
Our business calls. We cannot linger.
Let us go down while still the light is clear.

[Exit.]

[Enter Caissa below.]

Caissa: Oh, sorrowing the eyes that see
What this day I have seen! How leaden now
With grief this tongue of mine which must still tell
Into a royal ear a tale to split the heart.
For how can I now to the queen or to the buzzing hive
And say out bold what thing has passed this hour?
What's here? Oh, where have I now come to?
My terror's haste and too distracted state
Have carried me in ways I would not walk.
I think this is the very spot that band
Of brigands used. Oh, how may I ascend
And gain the road that runs into the town?
Yet cease, Caissa, cease. And listen now.

No, nothing. Gone. Perhaps a wild saluki dog
Makes howling to his distant mate. But hist!
Oh, fearful sound! What can this cry of anguish mean?
Such voice was never given to a man.
I've heard, yes sometime I have heard it told,
How ghostly figures skite abroad the land
In evil times, and evil times have come.
I'll take my refuge in this cave, that dark within
May hide me from some darker thing without.

[She hides within the cave.]

[Enter Polysemous and Xanthicus below.]

Polysemous: See, here before us lies our labor.
When we have lugged this crucible of bronze into the groves,
We will restore those men who now are sadly changed.

Xanthicus: I think were best if we must carry it
Some distance, as I fear, we make good use
The sturdy branches of that olive tree.

Polysemous: It is a fit suggestion, but I've another thought.
I'll warrant in the peddler's cart we'll find
An implement or some contrivance to the purpose.

Xanthicus: I'll look to it. Now this is strange.

Polysemous: Is there a bearing pole?

Xanthicus: Yet here's another.

Polysemous: What have you found?

Xanthicus: Each sack, each jar, and every merchandise
That's stowed here in this trap is hollow
Or is filled with tattered rags of stuff.

Polysemous: The peddler's poverty is most extreme.
Yet there; what is that there beyond the barrel?

Xanthicus: It seems a pike or gaff for fishing with.

Polysemous: Come, draw it out, and to our errand.

Xanthicus: And when we've born this cauldron thence, what then?
What is this art that will make men of beasts?

Polysemous: While we were on the way, my master,
Prince Telegonos, drew me aside the rest
Near one of those broken images of men

That stand in shattered disarray and guard
The greening slopes above us here.
There, he instructed me to chant a karakia
Which well attracts enchanted souls as once
The magic lyre of Amphion moved stones
To raise the walls of Thebes.

Xanthicus: But hush! Caution!
I hear it once again, now close at hand.

Polysemous: Let us make speed.

Xanthicus: You see, I'm not beguiled in this.

Polysemous: I know not what I heard. Nor does it matter
For this I know, that car once Phaeton drove
To close destruction of the world in fire
Is sinking in the west. Soon darkness comes.
We must these paths while still we have the light.

[Enter Calidus with drawn sword.]

Calidus: You there!

Polysemous: What's this?

Calidus: Stand fast!

Xanthicus: Beware his blade!

Calidus: It is well spoken that. Beware my blade in truth.
Stand fast, I say, for I am swift of foot.
I knew that I should find you by this spring,
That tainted wound within the side of the earth.

Xanthicus: It's but a fountain, sir.

Calidus: No, no, not so;
I say it is a very jet of blood.

Polysemous: What are these mad and lossy words you speak?

TELEGONOS, ACT IV

Calidus: I am not mad. But I have drained to dregs
A poisoned cup and am now drunk as with
An aconite of hate. So then, beware my blade!

Polysemous: I will abide you here. For comes to hand
This staff, which is though but a weapon crude,
It will suffice to keep a dog at bay.

[They fight.]

Calidus: I am no dog. Today I am a wolf.

Polysemous: See how he dodges back as if this were
That dancing floor which Daedalus once built.

Calidus: Such gigues I am well skilled at. I know a step
Will whirl you from the world of breathing men.

Polysemous: Yet seems your footing's not so sure for all of that.

Calidus: I'll write these outland jibes of yours
Upon the stones they'll use to raise your cairn.

Polysemous: Ha, growl wolf! My cudgel's tooth will teach you other.

Xanthicus: Mind well his grasp!

[He disarms Polysemous.]

Calidus: See how but a little twist disarms
And strips away fond hope. Clasp not my knees!
I am not one that you may supplicate.

Polysemous: Soldier, by all the gods, I pray you, spare!

Calidus: Did you not hear? I will delay no more.

Xanthicus: But why must it be so? Have mercy, sir!

Calidus: Mercy! Oh, once was mercy sweet to me,
More sweet was not wild honey off the comb!

But death must come to all. And now to you. Weep not
For greater men have passed this way before you.

Xanthicus: No, wait!

Calidus: Be silent, boy, and learn what death is.

[He makes as if to execute Polysemous, then, with a cry, casts away his sword and weeps.]

Too weak and far too brittle is my soul
For warlike deeds! Another arm than mine
Must take just vengeance for his slaughter then.

[Caissa creeps from the cave and attempts to exit unnoticed.]

Polysemous: What word is this?
     Whose slaughter, man? Come, speak.
No, I can stand, though shaken to the core.
Give me some answer now. Will you not speak?

Calidus: Now riven is the kingdom and our strength
And shattered is my heart. A ruined wall!
Once might I call myself a man, but now no more,
For he is dead to whom I owe my duty,
And I cannot give justice to his shade.

Polysemous: But who is dead?

Xanthicus: Did I not say from first
This island is an evil place where madness rules?
He raves. Pay him no mind.

Polysemous: Although his talk
Is of a frenzied sort, it hides some truth.

[He takes up the sword.]

Oh servant to the king, give heed my speech.
You seem a man in whom a kind
Of prudence dwells, and yet in this small thing

TELEGONOS, ACT IV

You were not wise, to cast away your sword.
It were a better course to save your mercy for your friends.
Speak now, be quick, and tell me who is dead.

Calidus: The king.

Polysemous: What said you there?

Calidus: I tell you plain,
In plain unpatterned words, the king is dead,
And what is more, by your own master's hand.

Polysemous: Telegonos has slain the king? You lie!

Calidus: It's truth! I swear by all the gods there are.

[After Caissa's discovery, Calidus exits unnoticed.]

Xanthicus: Behind!

Polysemous: Who's there?

Caissa: Ai Ai! Ah!

Polysemous: Come out from there!
Come out, I say, or this lament shall be
Your final utterance.

Xanthicus: It's but a maid.

Polysemous: A shepherd girl, I'd say. But, too, perhaps
She spies on what we're at. What make you here?

Caissa: Oh, be entreated, sir, I am no spy.
I took no part, but only watched from far
And worked no harm against your master prince.

Polysemous: What harm? I do not follow.

Caissa: I'll say no more.

Polysemous: No, no, I here adjure you tell your tale.

Xanthicus: He's gone.

Polysemous: What's that?

Xanthicus: While we were turned, he slipped
Among the rocks and fled away unmarked.
Shall I now give pursuit?

Polysemous: No, let him go.
It seems the girl has knowledge of these strange events.
Tell me, what is your name?

Caissa: Caissa, sir.

Polysemous: Caissa, listen closely to my words
You need not fear if you will speak but truth,
For I acquainted am with magic arts
And will well know it if a lie is told.

Caissa: I understand.

Polysemous: It seems my master, Prince Telegonos,
Has done some hurt against this island's king.
Is it not so?

Caissa: Yes sir, but—

Polysemous: You saw it then?

Caissa: I did, and yet I know not what I saw.

Polysemous: Strange words.

Caissa: Was most a stranger hour.

Polysemous: Just so.
Unfold to me, Caissa, now the whole
And keep not back the smallest patch or cutting.

Caissa: Then listen well to that which I relate.
I am a shepherdess, as you have rightly guessed,
And often shift my flocks on Neriton
Above us here. A festival is close,
And certain errand in that cause drew me
This day to leave my charges on the green
Within another's care. And so immersed
In happy plans and visions of the day,
I walked through alder copses to the town
And worked a gentle chain of tansy flowers
That I might wear in garland to the feast.
Ours is no country fit for driving horses,
And all our footpaths never travel straight.
Even those native born can lose their way,
And so it was with me that fated hour,
When turning at a little crossroad Herme,
Came to my eyes a sight. My lord the king,
Disguised in garments of a peddler man,
Played as a guide to company of four;
An ancient one with staff and beggared rags,
Yourself, the boy, and him that you call prince.
When you went back beside the mossy ford,
Entranced on such a spectacle unheard,
I followed still but kept a certain farness back
And tended to their path among the spikes of corn.

Polysemous: Oh, by the gods! The peddler was the king himself!
I knew it not, but wholly was deceived!
But yet resume the tale and halt not 'til the end.

Caissa: There lies a vale by Arethusa's spring
Where stands an old abandoned hut of stone.
Longwhile ago it was of prospect wide,
But since the forest has grown close about.
And to this place decayed, deserted, and
So desolate my lord the king brought hither
That beggar and your prince, while I, concealed
Behind a stand of elm and whitethorn trees, gazed on.
When come within that rubbled fence of stone,
The king gave forth a whistled signal call
At which leaped forth an ordered company

Of soldiers armed. And though your prince gave valiant fight,
In swiftest time their numbers had prevailed.
Then were your lord and too that ancient sire
Bound hard against a gibbet's timber post.
I watched as were a pantomime before me played,
While with malicious, black, and angered looks, the king
Paced forth and back and seemed to give harangue
And then to question and then to threat your prince.
Who answered not but kept his silence well.
But sudden came a stir among the gathered men
At which a herald called the king to view
Such marvel as I've never seen before.
A stag as white as is the mist of sea
Paced calm into the midst of men
And stared about with reason in his eye.
My lord the king, who loves to hunt the buck,
Took up your master's spear and motion made
As readied for the cast.

                                      Oh, that I had
Been born without the taste of light than to
Have seen what followed by that shanty next.
For sudden cry gave out that ancient man,
Who must have been, I think, of wizard-kind.
And yet, it was not cry, but still a kind of song,
Which tore apart the sky.
Then flames descended from the great above
And harmed them not but burnt their bonds to twists.
Sprang forth your prince and grappled close the king
And wrenched the spear but could not gain it thus.
Confusion and disorder overcame
The well-greaved soldiers standing 'round about.
Maddened, as by a magic spell, they drew
Their swords and rushed now friend against his friend.
Still there amid such butchery, your prince
Yet struggled hard and wrestled with the king,
Until with final desperate lunge, he hauled
His weapon free. Down plunged the spear, and dark
With blood grew breast and temple of the king.
And having witnessed there what I should not,
In terror so I fled from out that place

To bear the daughter of Icarius this word.
Now you have heard the tale I have to tell
You have been patient, sir, be merciful as well.

Polysemous: For this good word you shall go free indeed!
This is the best of news that you have told,
And my troubled heart takes much delight at it.
Telegonos has slain the king! It's true!

Caissa: Before I go, I will a caution speak.
It is not wise to vaunt so on the downfall
Of your adversary. Think too on this,
That fallen now is Ithaca the great,
Whose fame once spread even to the land of Troy.
Yield reverence, sir. It would be better so.

Polysemous: That name! That name! Halt there!
      Why spoke you now that name?

Caissa: I do not understand you.

Xanthicus: Be peaceable, sir
And let her go her way as you have said.

Polysemous: It cannot be, and yet I fear is so.
I will be true my pledge. You soon may leave
But first I urge you to relate a thing.
What is this kingdom's name?

Caissa: Oh, miserable!
The conqueror that recks not his domain.
Know then, stranger, that you have come to rocky Ithaca
Where lately ruled lord king Odysseus,
Who as the story runs sacked Priam's town,
But now is dead and no more than a name.

[Exit.]

Polysemous: Oh, savage truth, that men should never bear!

Xanthicus: Odysseus, the father that he sought!

Polysemous: This wind shall dash his fondest hope
And tumble down my fortunes with his own.
I cannot take it in.

Xanthicus: I am the same.
He knew it then, by tokens and by signs,
But I dissuaded him against it.

Polysemous: What's this? Do you now weep?

Xanthicus: How shall I not?
For much it pangs my heart to think upon his case.

Polysemous: You are too impressible. Cease now.
It were a better hour to lay our plans.
Bear up, I say! For I have need of you.

Xanthicus: What shall we do?

Polysemous: Be silent while I think.
My heart is blank as is the sky of nights
When overcast within the dark of the moon.

Xanthicus: We should to him and make the matter known
That we may share some part in his affliction.

Polysemous: It would be ill. I have another counsel.

Xanthicus: I'll hear it.

Polysemous: This theme within our minds
Is uppermost, Telegonos has slain
His sire, the good and object of his search.

Xanthicus: So far, I follow in the wake you cut.

Polysemous: But him that fled and too that shepherdess
To all my best of estimation
Have flown as straight as cranes from off a winter marsh
To seek the citadel and tell this island's queen.
Majesty will view a different facet here,

TELEGONOS, ACT IV

That we are party to a regicide
And things of crime that she may wish to hunt.

Xanthicus: I had not given thought to such as this.
Your words sharp up the edge of all my fears.

Polysemous: We must now stay to our first purpose sure;
Transforming those who now are changed to beasts
That we may win some ally to our cause.

Xanthicus: You do say right in this. Take up our task.
We'll bear this magic herb into the forest dense.

Polysemous: That from such evil we may bring about a good.

[Exit.]

[Enter below Telegonos driving Odysseus bound before him. The king has bloody bandages at his temple and chest.]

Telegonos: There, down upon the shingle of this strand
And cease your howling, dog, though soon enough
You will have rest of other and eternal sort.

Odysseus: If you would do me murder, make swift,
For I am wracked as by an agony of fire.

Telegonos: It seems you have forgot the tale I told;
Already has my javelin brought death
Into your blood. Sometime I have observed
In chasings of the hunt the venom works
Now quick, now slow, or takes a middle course,
But will inevitable, in subject time,
As waves must break when once they take their rise,
Bring sleep from which there is then no awaking.
Yet in such captive moments that remains you,
I'll bind the harvest of your mind in shocks of speech.

Odysseus: How is it just that I have come to this?
And where immortal gods your aid now need is near?
What savage incantation of my enemies

Called down this fate? Once I was noble and a king
And tasted every simple of joy earth;
The sweet companionship of hero friends,
Great deeds of arms, and work that conquers all.
I loved a wife and fought my way from far
Against the wastes of sea to make return to her
And to my loving son and only heir.
Now all is cancelled, lost, and gone from me,
As though it were a page deleted, erased,
And blotted out by mending of a careless scribe.
It is not fit that I should die unanswered so
Amid these fragments of a broken world.
How has this come about? How have I come to this?

Telegonos: On other themes than these I'd hear you speak
For I have only made a fit requital
Against such treachery you practiced.

Odysseus: What is this place?

Telegonos: It is the beach where late
You played your tinker part. But speak!
Too long have I wound out with weary steps
The labyrinth course of all your many lies.
What is your name, Oh king?

Odysseus: I have been here before.
So cold! How desolate this cavern vast,
And littered with the leavings of the dead.

Telegonos: Think not by freshly minted fictions
That you will shift me from pursuit of truth.
Yield now! For I have fairly won the day.

Odysseus: See here, a rusted skull
Has rested through some countless pass of years,
And there, the fretwork of a sailor's ribs
Who lost both way and life in other days.

Telegonos: These are but stones and brands and wreckages of wood!

TELEGONOS, ACT IV

Odysseus: So cold! It freezes me with burning fire.
Here no wind blows. No stock of green can trace its path
Across these sheer and rifted granite sides.
This vaulted roof of rock shuts out the light
Dragged down! Buried alive! Interred! Entombed!
Within this stony chamber of the earth!
I know this place. I have been here before.

Telegonos: I think he does not feign it. The poisoned taint
Has reached into his brain, and now his mind paints out
This scene from memory of times that have passed by.
His sanity is shattered as a glass.

Odysseus: I hear his ragged breath. He comes.

Telegonos: Who comes, old man?

Odysseus: The cyclops! The cyclops comes! He comes!
Oh, horrible! Oh, would that I could make escape by trickery
But strength has fled away and ebbed my limbs.

Telegonos: How miserable to see his reason overthrown!
Had he but died still in his regal pride,
And mantled with a robe of arrogance,
I might have felt contempt, but no regret.
But now this abject madness tears my heart.

Odysseus: See how it shambles forth the darkness
And halts to balance on the ball its fist,
Tilting back with narrow head to snuff
The stagnant air! Oh gods, the horror of it!
Now with a single gaze, weird as a cuttlefish,
It fixes me, thrusts forward, lumbering,
To spill the blood my life like melted lead.
Ha! Who's there? Oh, wondrous joy! I may yet still be saved!

Telegonos: Note how his mind in vain delusion shifts.
What do you see, Oh King, that you rejoice?

Odysseus: Salvation comes! The beast's advance is checked
Checked by the action of a single warrior bold

Who lunges with a lance for fighting on the sea.
It is Libanos now as I perceive.
Ho there, Libanos, who rules to bring about reform in men!
He now is joined by company of three
Who kneel in archer pose to loose their deadly shafts.
The fair haired Smyrna shoots, then Calamus lets fly.
A third, whose face is hidden by the grain of light,
Must be that noble Alahoth who governs
On the island shores of Enkrateia's realm.
Oh, great deliverance! They've driven back the beast,
Which shields its face by milling of its arms.
But hold, hold, victory is not yet come,
Though still I have a burning cause for hope.

Telegonos: This sickness of the mind makes sick my heart
I cannot stand to listen to these ravings more.

Odysseus: Ah, now it rises up the fullness of its height
And tipping back that so misshapen head
Gives vent to rage in bellow like a bull,
Then plunges sudden forward to the charge.
But here, enduring Krokos dashes in the fight,
To plant his pike in fracture of the rock
And so impales the beast with its own weight.
Oh, by immortal gods! See how it yerks
And struggles, close to death. Now comes a band
Of other heroes swift to so enforce on it its end.
Comes Nardos with a gaze serene but much
Determined in his will. And Camphyre who
Rejoices greatly in the battle fierce.
And though this image now dissolves,
I think by this one's gait it's Kinnamon,
Who's never tardy to some action good.
Comes striding on one warrior last, who never fails,
And pierces with his sword the cyclops's heart
But ah! Flap, flap! Flep, flep! As when a scroll's wound up,
I reel, and light of other days fades out the scene.
Flap, flap! Flep, flep! The wax is broke, and all is turned to dust.

Telegonos: See how he slumps down to the earth. I think he's gone.

TELEGONOS, ACT IV

Odysseus: What's this? Still here, carrion prince?

Telegonos: I thought you had already crossed the river.

Odysseus: While I draw breath, I am still ruler here.
Fetch me a drink from out this spring to cool
My burning tongue.

Telegonos: Not from respect your office,
I'll damp this cloth that you may sip a little.

Odysseus: Too late, I feel a final agony!
So dies Odysseus, who sacked the city Troy!

Telegonos: That name!

Odysseus: I am Odysseus, I say!
And by my greatness have deserved a death
Of other sort than this. But no, wait, wait!
If this is to exact—

[He dies.]

Telegonos: Father!

But no.

Now have I gained so too, now have I lost,
All in one swift turning of a phrase.

How instant I am perfect in my desolation!
For as the sun sinks down beneath the rim of ocean,
Deep darkness falls across this island and my heart
And brings a silence vaster than the sky.
If I could sing a hymn with voice of Orpheus,
Who as the story's told made stones to weep,
Then only might I tell to all the earth
And cause them hear the magnitude my grief.
But I have no such remedy of words,
And is no tongue in all the lands of men
Could catch or could express the sound my sorrow makes.

I've killed the father that I sought!
Oh, who will strip away this ugly mask
That I have now become? Such work could no man do,
And yet I do not know of any god
Who cares for such a task as this.
Father, what have I now to offer you but tears?
But hear! Perhaps some folk come hence!
I must now hide myself away from searching eyes of men.
Away, Telegonos! Away!
My heart! My heart! My heart!

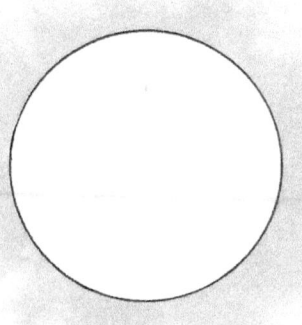

ACT V

Same scene. Night with fog.

[Enter soldiers bearing torches followed by a captain.]

Captain: Soldier, what news of the night?

1st Soldier: None but the worst.
Those sons of jades who speak commands in safety
Know nothing, say less, and are but villainous.

Captain: I am a captain sent from out the castle.
What car is that? Go up and make a search
That none may steal upon us unawares.

2nd Soldier: It is most prudent. I'll look to it.

Captain: Hard is the lot of those who serve the god of war,
But be afraid to vent such rude disorders.
Come hither close and haste to give report.

1st Soldier: Your pardon, noble sir.
I did not know you in this fog that scums
The wicked earth. I'm most surprised
To find you in thick with honest men
Who mow with bloody sickles in the fields of war.

Captain: Enough. Leave off this bitter insolence.
For I would learn the sum of your account.

1st Soldier: Then you shall hear of terrors to daunt a stalwart heart.
When in the ruddy hour the sun declines,
We marched from out the precincts of the town
And vaunted much the prowess of our skill.
But coming to the hovel kept some yesterings
By that misfortuned son of Ktesios,
We found beneath the moon a scene of horror.
Our brothers and our sons, the flower of Ithaca,
Lay stark and dead whatever place they fell.
Here hands that rattled once the noble spear
Clutch at the dust and nevermore shall move
And eyes that yesterday beheld fair martial deeds
Are now struck blind, to stare forever sightless on the earth.

Captain: Have never seen a ground of battle then?
For fierce Bellona shall make a peaceful grove
To sweat with blood. What of the adversary
That did this wickedness?

1st Soldier: Hold fast, good captain.
For you have yet to hear the pinnacle
And zenith of the tale. For clear it was
To any viewed the scene, none other force
Our honored dead encountered in that vale.
For friend had grappled close with friend to slay
Their mates as they lay dying. Such snarls, such fury,
Such mad contorted visages I hope,
By savage gods, to never see again.
As if all wicked passions that most are pent within
Were written large upon each countenance.
A final silence hangs the air to rend
The heart like strange and soundless music.
I'm not a man to start at any hob,
Yet not the warlike fray nor clash of arms
Destroyed our host, but potent sorcery.

Captain: Be calm. The world is filled with such like happenstance,
For there are realms invisible to men.
What have you found to make so swift return?

2nd Soldier: It seems some market chapman in his haste
Has left behind his wain and spilled its cartage.
But see, what deal of lossy stuff he cries?

Captain: We learn then nothing new from him.
Though but this wizardry is fearful,
I'm much relieved to find the enemy
We marched to seek is but a boojum of the mind.
What news of king Odysseus whom you
Were sent to seek?

1st Soldier: Stay yet again, good captain,
I pray you, stay. For I must punctuate
This sad event, as by an epilogue.
Of our dread majesty, the son of Laertes,

We nothing learned with any certainty.
Yet while we gazed upon this too enchanted scene,
Some simple folk from out the greenwood copse
Made known to us the nature of our foemen.
For with much gibberish of their rude yawping,
They told how they had spied a company of beasts
That gathered to a hollow of the glen.
A steaming cauldron there was set,
And each that smoking liquor drank rose up,
Transformed before their eyes, to warlike men at arms.
Then this new minted soldiery, much like
Those Myrmidons that served the fleet Achilles,
Howled out to wound our city and our land.

Captain: And do you yield your credence to this tale?
Have seen these beastmen or tracked upon their course?

1st Soldier: Some sights we've had but through the mist,
As shifting figures in a shifting sense,
For fog rolls in from off the ocean
And tricks the world in rags of mystery.

[Enter scout at left.]

Captain: What man is that who comes?!

Scout: Who challenges?!

Captain: I am a captain and soldier of the king!

Scout: I am a scout. Stand down, that I may hasten over!

Captain: Approach, that we may know you!

1st Soldier: I mark his voice.
It is the sentry posted to the brae.

Captain: Good then. For I like not to be in ignorance.

Scout: Ai! Ai! Ah!

Captain: What troubles you? Ho there, speak out!

Scout: A man lies here.

Captain: What's that he said? For I caught not the sense.

1st Soldier: He has discovered there some hindrance.

Captain: Hold fast, and we will cross to you. Be wary still.
On such a circumstance were best if we are cautious.

1st Soldier: Agreed. This night is inexplicable.

[They cross to center.]

Captain: Well met. Now say what man you are.

Scout: I am such one who makes intelligence of arms.
Scant news I have to match this warlike cause,
Yet at our feet lies something more obscure.

2nd Soldier: By Hecate and all the deathless gods!

Captain: Do not start back. Have never seen a corse?
He seems a peddler man done in by violence.

Scout: Ha, are you sure?

Captain: It is a common end.
How many hundred are about the land
To cant their fabled wares in every town?
Would that the crown should send them bleating hence.

Scout: But stay, my friend. Observe and mark him close.

1st Soldier: Captain, as I breathe, it is the king!

Captain: What foolish talk is this? Be silent.

Scout: Though impudent, he speaks the truth.

TELEGONOS, ACT V

Captain: The truth? Then you are of this same opinion?

Scout: Opinion, do you say?

Captain: It can be nothing else.
Or but some fine fantastic whimsy of the mind.

Scout: By signs and certain proofs I know this is the king.

Captain: A shadow falls across his face. Stand back.
Stand back, I say, and keep the light steady.
I will admit he bears a passing semblance to our lord,
Yet this may only be the tender of appearance.
Glance back and you will see a peddler cart,
Abandoned recent in some hasty spur.
Look there, what tatty stuff he wears.
See here, this cloth from off the wain.
Matched side by side, in sum, they are the same.
And thus, as solid as the form of truth,
He more partakes the peddler than the king.

1st Soldier: Do you mistrust your eyes? It is the king!

Captain: Be silent now, I say. The truth of things
Lies often far from our experience.

Scout: You are too absolute. Come, let me reason you.
This man was one eye blind, just as our lord
Since he contended at Thesprotis.
And as a writing on his thigh that scar,
That famous scar, he took, or so they say,
When on Parnassus in the prime of youth.
Now adding up these accidents to the account,
As when a soldier stands against the fleeing route,
Presents me with a certainty; it is our lord.
You there, is it not plain to proof that we have found the king?

2nd Soldier: I'm not a man who's practiced in debate,
But seems it to my thought most unadorned
That the world is as we may conceive it,
So as we're taught our duty we may act.

Scout: What's answer's this? I do not comprehend.
Is it the king, or no? Speak to the issue, man.

[A cry from offstage.]

Voice: Hear! Hear! A signal sounds the air!
       The queen approaches!

Captain: The queen, you say? Too rough, the situation!
Say nothing on this mystery, I charge you.

[Enter Penelope born on an open palanquin with attendants.]

Penelope: Halt here my car that I may speak with these.

Captain: Down now before the daughter of Icarius!
Most sovereign Queen, we wait on your command.

Penelope: These are fair words to hear. Would that the prospect
Were likewise fair and all the world at peace.
Come rise up now, that we may best convey the time.

Captain: We were but lately advertised, your majesty,
Of this too sudden progress through the land,
And much it fears my heart to see you here.

Penelope: Since your late dispatch to the field in haste
A grave event has clashed across the land.

Captain: What is the fine of it that I may better serve you?

Penelope: Learn then how our situation stands.
Although convinced by some confused report
To make defense against vague enemies without,
The enemy within proved greater far.
The raw ungoverned multitude,
Hearing whispered tales and rumors
On the theme that great Odysseus was dead,
Spoke first from house to house against the king,
Then gathered in each lane and public square,
'Til by the mutual transformation of their hate

They grew into a mob. And now, entranced
By dreams of dignity and of freedom,
They have convulsed the state to anarchy.

Captain: I see now reason to your urgent haste.
We shall return and make these renegades—

Penelope: Stay, captain, stay. I choose another course.

Scout: My Queen, you cannot let rebellion thrive.
Such vices merit hard necessity,
Decisive force, and punishment of arms.

Penelope: Or else some policy more subtle.
But far too soon and too disorderly the night
To so invent a sound machinery of words.
I will across the bridge in secrecy,
Come to the haven by the shortest way,
Take ship, and sail for Samos with the dawn.
My son, the prince Telemachus, is there
And from that sanctuary place we may devise
And seek hard after news of King Odysseus.

2nd Soldier: Alarm! Alarm! Take up your weapons!
An adversary force approaches.

Captain: Look to the queen! Look to the queen! We will defend.
My sight is made imperfect by the mist.
How far? What is their strength? And how are they appointed.

1st Soldier: I caught but most a fragmentary glance
As they passed through some falling in the light,
But I surmise they're half a hundred strong,
And each man carried in his hand an implement of war.

Captain: You think them rioters from out the city, then?

2nd Soldier: They bear themselves more soldierly
And make with steady purpose for this place.

Captain: Your majesty, I bid you to remove

And seek a safe retreat. We are but few,
And is the main our force some distance yet.

Polysemous: [*From offstage.*]
Hold hard! Hold hard, you soldiers of the king, and hear me!

Captain: Who calls?

Polysemous: A one yet holds a cutting of dispute
But would the more contend with words than swords.
Will you hear me?

Scout: He bids us to a parley.

Captain: If one of you lays down his arms, he may come hither.

Polysemous: You shield behind a personage of rank.
I'd speak with her and none besides.

Penelope: I'll hear his talk.

Scout: It is too dangerous, my lady.

Penelope: Such passages require a bolder front.
We will make show of confidence and trust him.

[*Enter Polysemous.*]

Polysemous: I lay down here the weapon that I bear and come.

Captain: Tell those behind to beat out a chamade,
That all may know we parley.

[*He crosses to Penelope.*]

Polysemous: Great Queen Penelope,
I touch your feet and kneel before you as a suppliant.

Penelope: Save ceremony such as this for some far less
Endangered hour. Who are you men that come
Like criminals from out the closeness of the night?

Polysemous: My name is called Polysemous
And that I may prevent some further bloodshed
I beg your leave to speak. For strange events
Have driven us to take up warlike arms.

Penelope: Say on, but in this charge be brief.

Polysemous: Most Sovereign Queen,
      by some contingent drift of chance
I think you have but late become acquainted
On this sad fact which grieves the very stars
That great Odysseus, Laertes' son, is dead.

Penelope: I have the while no steadfast certainty
But echoes of this tale have reached into my house.
And how are you caught up in skeins of the event?

Polysemous: I am a man once was some part nobility
But lately serve the son of Circe called Telegonos.

Penelope: With Circe, daughter of the Sun, I am acquainted.
But your Telegonos is quite unknown to me.
Still yet proceed and haste to make the matter known,
For time is often ally to the bold.

Polysemous: I'm not a man to flinch away the truth
So shall I go most straightly to the purpose.
This prince Telegonos I served of late
Claimed also to some kinship with your lord,
And from the spur of this presumption,
He drove out on the restless tides of ocean
To seek this island Ithaca. But late
Our vessel foundered, and we came forth in ignorance
That we had lighted on the object of our search.

Not half a stage from hence, there lies a greening field,
Pent up with rocky walls for keeping in the cattle.
There came Prince Telegonos and I along some else,
And thought, in our distress, to raid the herd.
Your lord, the great Odysseus, was passing by
And came to give defense or drive us off,

Yet stayed my prince relentless to this cause.
There beneath a troubled ruck of umber cloud,
These valiant heroes would not turn or yield,
But gave out stroke for bloody stroke,
Until, as goes the sad tale of world,
The youth prevailed and struck him down.
As he lay dying, still regal though now fallen in the dust,
We learned who we had slain. Then this Telegonos,
In abject terror of the Kindly Ones
Or laws of honest men, fled out in haste
And passes from the substance of this tale.

We few who here remained have taken up these arms
But for defense and throw ourselves upon your mercy.
If shall your majesty see fit to ratify
A clement treaty with us on this theme,
We will depart out your domains in peace.

Penelope: You are a very rogue who speaks not straight!
Or else you twist the case to fill up some design.
But by my life, you said your part most bravely.
And in my much experience of years,
I've found that truth is often as the state would make it known.
Some called my husband King Odysseus a tyrant,
Yet for my part I will not stain his memory,
For he was kind to me. But what of this
Telegonos, this prince you claim serve?

Polysemous: Though once I counted him a friend,
I have but little hope, and so I make my way
Best as I can against a fitful world.

Penelope: Hear then the terms that I shall stipulate.
If you so draw your force around this hill
To meet our gathered army in the glen,
Lay down your warlike arms in one accord,
Our troop will then convey you the port,
Where you may voyage out from Ithaca.
My route lies also on the same tonight,
And if you grant when we are private,
I'll speak a word or two to your advantage.

TELEGONOS, ACT V

Polysemous: I give consent to all that you have said.

Penelope: Then we are reconciled, and will rejoin
Our converse when the time is opportune.

Polysemous: I take my leave of you with reverency and thanks.

[Exit Polysemous.]

Penelope: Raise up my car and sign them halt until I come.
I bid you, Captain, follow on behind
To keep in vigilance the sight of our retreat.

Captain: I will, Oh Queen, make caution to obey.

[Exit Penelope.]

Scout: How are you minded, sir, concerning this?

Captain: Such matter is too high for me to know.
As to the shoot of our first controversy,
Take up the carcass there, that we may bear it hence.
When by a little space we can withdraw,
We may resume the argument and seek the truth.

2nd Soldier: How strange an hour that we should march in amity
With that same enemy we sought to conquer.
These beastmen are most civilized.

1st Soldier: Did you not hear? They were but servants to a prince.

2nd Soldier: Hup, now! A king, or no, he is a royal burden.
Still he who makes himself as lowly as a worm durst not
Complain when he is trodden on.

Captain: March on, that we may gain the haven with the light.

[Exit carrying the body of Odysseus.]

[Enter Kalonous above carrying a stock of wood.]

Kalonous: How friendless is the night to travelers
Who walk with wounded steps and have no home,
Yet is this night more friendless to me still,
Who have but lately waked from nightmares of the flesh.
Am I a man? Are these again my own true hands
That were so recent cleft to canter on the earth?
As though I did but dream it, that we cast off
The goddess' isle, and sudden am restored.
Now some assassin dogs my steps as would a shadow.
But, by the Horseman! Never have I played a coward's part!
In truth, these are my own rough hands again.
This stock is but a cudgel crude, yet it shall serve me,
So here I will abide to teach how hard
An old man's hands may be.

[Enter Xanthicus. At some time during the following exchange, Telegonos enters above unnoticed above, walking slowly as if in a dream and stops hidden from their view.]

Kalonous: Come closer, sly foot!
For I would question you. Though age has frosted me,
My blood is running fire!

Xanthicus: No, do not strike me!

Kalonous: What man are you who so pursues me through the dark?!

Xanthicus: Be more peaceable! I but mistook you.

Kalonous: So much is evident. You thought to steal
Me unawares, but I am sharper in my sense.

Xanthicus: A passing likeness but deceived my sense.

Kalonous: You doubtless seek some victim in this welter.

Xanthicus: Not so, a prince. A youthful prince.

Kalonous: That you may murder him?!

Xanthicus: I swear by all the gods, you do me wrong!

Kalonous: By thunder, look me in the eye that I may certify
You speak no word to me but truth!

Xanthicus: I know you!

Kalonous: How's this? From whence? For I am foreign born.

Xanthicus: Are you not that one called Kalonous
Who lately sailed from Circe's dreaded isle
And by her magic arts was changed into a stag?

Kalonous: I am that man you name. How do you know me?

Xanthicus: The one I seek is Prince Telegonos.
He is my friend. I hope to give him aid.

Kalonous: For sport a man might speak the same,
But by your gaze I think you are an honest youth.
Now am I prompt to recognize you,
Who entered in the greenwood shaw with herbs,
That proved the means of great deliverance
To creatures mute yet with the eyes of men.

Xanthicus: How is it, sir, that you go not with them?

Kalonous: I had no stomach for it. For did you not observe
When we resumed our former humanness,
That traitor called Polysemous conferred
In private speech and then with Thymos at his side,
By some facility of pretty words,
Inflamed the rest against the prince?
But to Telegonos, I owe a debt of loyalty.
If truly as you say you seek for him,
Then let us act as together on this cause.

Xanthicus: Such comradeship you offer is most welcome,
For I am weary.

Telegonos: One light.

Xanthicus: I hear a sound.

Kalonous: It's but a drum that beats out cadence to a march.

Xanthicus: Yet something else there is as well.

Telegonos: And undivided.

Kalonous: Be hist! Draw back within this gut of rock
That we may gain a breathing moment.

Xanthicus: What is this new misfortune has occurred?

Kalonous: A figure stands close by with face avert
To gaze the darkness of the troubled sea
As one entranced. Scarce can I say
Why should be so, this sight brims up my heart
With awe and holy dread. Though still the night
Holds all the land as in a mouth of shadow,
It seemed we had strayed forth to tread bright wonderlands
Where never sets the golden day.

Xanthicus: I would myself see such a prodigy.

Kalonous: Has he withdrawn, or does he stand the same?

Xanthicus: Though he is voiceless as a logan stone,
It's as he speaks rare mysteries in language of a dream.
Yet something certifies my sense, it is the prince.

Kalonous: 'Spite that I am as one amazed on it,
By Thrax, you strike the thought of my own heart!

Xanthicus: Shall we advance on him?

Kalonous: But cautiously.

[They approach.]

Kalonous: I am convinced beyond a shade of doubt.
What's this? Rise up. Why do you kneel?

Xanthicus: Halt here. No further step I pray you,

For I am overset by my vehement terror.

Kalonous: Be calm. I'll make a trial and speak to him.
Hail, silent apparition of the night.
Are you that one men name as Prince Telegonos?
Or, if you are some eidolon of shadow,
We crave you tell us where he may be found.

Xanthicus: He does not heed or seem to hear us.

Kalonous: Oh, you who stand in stillness thus before us,
Will you not speak or yield to us some sign?
For by your countenance, you are that one we seek.

Xanthicus: Oh, come, my prince, and we shall lead you hence.

Telegonos: Peace, peace. I know you, friend. Give me your hand.

Kalonous: Ah, Prince, I was in dread to see you stand
As one who is ensorcelled by a spell
And we have had strange visions of the mind.

Telegonos: What, here, Kalonous? And are the rest restored?

Kalonous: Polysemous has done as you have asked,
And each has now resumed his human shape.
But like a viper he has led them hence.

Telegonos: Perhaps this is the best. All shall be well.

Xanthicus: Oh Prince, will you not haste away this night
To be a guest within our village halls?

Telegonos: My pilgrimage lies now on other paths,
For I have made vow and must fulfill it.

Kalonous: What vow is this you speak on, sir?

Telegonos: If you would hear, I'll first say monstrous words
That no man living yet should have to speak,
For you must know my crime. But, no, I cannot speak it!

It is too horrible and scalds my throat!

Kalonous: Good prince—

Telegonos: Do not call me good!
I am a parricide and regicide, for in one stroke
I killed the king and father whom I sought!
Now I have said the whole. Look on me if you dare.

Xanthicus: You are my friend and I, for equal measure,
Would brave the anger of the vengeful gods.

Kalonous: For my son's sake and for my own I shall not waver
To journey at your side. And though you plunge
Like Orpheus to grieve and sing among the dead,
Then Kalonous will follow where you lead.

Telegonos: You are good comrades to my bitterness,
Yet shall I for a moment turn aside.
Most do I weep for him and for myself
And for your gentle words and for another's
For even in the sore of my distress,
A strange event has happened in the night
That gives new hope to men. But, to the stroke.
Do you yet wish to hear the tale I have to tell?

Kalonous: We do.

Telegonos: Then I will show, as in a burning mirror,
Bright images of truth.

Xanthicus: Say on, we will attend you.

Telegonos: When in that careful hour truth shattered me,
Fear drove me forth into the empty night.
Scarce in my reason then, I crossed a flat of barren clay
Where marched a sparse of wind tormented pines
To come among those blocks of stone above the ocean.
There, forcing passage through the bracken on the crown,
I found a gap that gave above the sea.
Longwhile I stood there in the darkness,

Revolving darker thoughts within my darkened mind.
Then overcome, compelled with weariness of grief,
I made a pillow of a nearby stone
And nestled down the dust and fell asleep.

As I descended spiring rifts of dream,
Came to my humming ear a voice that called my name.
Most well-beloved the speaker seemed to me,
So rising up the raveled jags of slumber,
I went forth clothed in splendor as a king
To make a stately progress by the sea.

Yet hindering our path before a mystery of sky
That ancient man who kept with us this day.
And he cried out that I might know him
For a messenger who served an Unknown God.
The haughty lords of rank who tended to my way
But mocked and laughed to see his poverty,
Yet I desired him say what god he meant.

In sober silence then that one raised up his staff
And gesture made that I should gaze upon the strand.
Hard by our place, I glimpsed a Wondrous Pearl,
That glowed with simple radiance
Which seemed but darkness to my frailty of sight
And filled my heart with peaceful terror.
For seemed it to my mind that I beheld
The fountain and the sum of every good.
Just as past time I once had yearned
To find this island Ithaca and know my father,
So then, I fervent burned most ardently
That I might gain the Pearl. But though I keenly longed,
The courtly throng in anger clutched my cloak
As scantly might I draw out breathe, but most I knew
That I could not approach that Holy One
Vested in the mantle of my kingly pride.
Whence wrenching free the hands that grasped me back
And casting down all togs of office
I crossed and knelt the shingle there beside.
For all these honored things of earth
Were nothing worth to me beside the Pearl.

In then but an instant through the folded drift of time
We floated 'mersed the tides of ocean.
No fear had I but glided peaceful as an owl,
Since by my side there stayed with me the Pearl.
For though these things took place
In but the semblance of a vision,
Most surely in that hour this Unknown God
In stillness spoke like gentle thunder to my heart.
I am the Father that you truly sought
In constant journey on the troubled sea.
Search out my kingdom in rising sun
And shall your crime in that day be healed and forgiven.

Thence while we thus communed,
As friend will speak with friend,
My substance changed, and I became a pearl,
In image of the image I beheld
And lived a thousand years within an hour.
Then dreaming was by winds of music blown,
And I came to myself and found I was alone.

Kalonous: What is this strange new deity that you announce?
This train strikes much astonishment in me!

Xanthicus: Will you then go beyond the lands of men?

Telegonos: I am an outcast to the shores of earth,
And though I bear my shame before a multitude,
As much as lies in me, I shall attempt it.
The line once brought division finds its end.
Foretimes had I servants many, now shall I serve
With sober gladness and joyous grief
In reverence to that Holy One I seek.

Kalonous: My Prince, this matter merits more consideration,
But to the present moment's need, were best
We leave this place and seek another coast.

Xanthicus: My vessel's small but will serve three in turn.

Telegonos: I will be so advised. Longwhile I sought

TELEGONOS, ACT V

This island kingdom of my father's stead,
But no more can I stay. Lie there, my lance,
For you proved too invincible for me.
Telegonos will after face the world,
A wanderer with nothing in his hands.
Where is the boat?

Xanthicus: Hard by that tail of rock.
I must a moment mend my sandal.
Begin the path, and I will hasten to you.

Telegonos: Do not be long for dawn is in the air.

[Exit Telegonos.]

Xanthicus: What is your judgement, sir, concerning this?

Kalonous: Judgement, you say? It's not a thing to judge.

Xanthicus: And yet your looks are skeptical, as though
He were demented by the greatness of his grief.

Kalonous: Be easy, lad. The world is intricate
And full of marvels. Never have I heard
The savage gods show mercy, for they are cruel.
And often in our grief, we see what we would see.
But I am old, and old men are more slow to meditate.
I must study at this ecstasy a while.
Let's to the prince, that he may find his way.
Why do you hesitate? What have you found?

Xanthicus: See what is here? In pyres of hyacinth
Some lowly worm has stricken through his husk
To join the bright imagines of the air
And nimble leave the bonds of earth.

Kalonous: Soon breaks the golden dawn. Let us be going.

The End

Jonathan Golding grew up in South East Asia as the son of Protestant missionaries. An avid reader, he developed an interest in writing early in life. He attended the University of La Verne, in Southern California, where he majored in literature and theater arts. Although he initially desired to imitate the works of modern and avant garde poets and novelists, he eventually found himself drawn to classical forms of expression. While researching the literature of late antiquity, he began reading the early Church Fathers. He converted to Eastern Orthodox Christianity in 2006. He currently resides in San Diego, California.

Previously, Golding contributed to ***Clearing Paths: A Darkly Bright Anthology of Verse*** (Darkly Bright Press, 2021).

Visit his website, *Worlds Imagined*: www.httpstextures.com.

Megan Elizabeth Gilbert received a BA in Fine Arts and Art Education from PLNU in San Diego, while also studying in France and Greece. She has taught art in Canada, the US, and Europe. She and her husband and their four children are currently residing at St. Vladimir's Orthodox Theological Seminary in New York.

You can view more of her work at www.megan-gilbert.com.

www.ingramcontent.com/pod-product-compliance
Lightning Source LLC
Chambersburg PA
CBHW060615080526
44585CB00013B/845